Write That Book And Make That Money;
Expert Strategies for The Hungry Author

By: LaShonda DeVaughn

LSDV Publications

Copyright ©2018 LSDV Publications

Printed in the United States of America 1 2 3 4 5 6 7 8 9 1 0

PUBLISHER'S NOTE:

Editor: LSDV Publications Editorial Services

In Loving Memory of Andre Stone...

Contents

Introduction

When I picked up my pen in 2007, never in my wildest dreams would I have ever imagined that I'd one day be the owner of my own publishing company; or create an entire brand based on my writing ability. I knew that I was on to something when I wrote my first book, but I didn't realize that I was on to something even bigger than myself. It literally seemed like it happened overnight. I went from staring at my thick, handwritten manuscript, scattered in my messy bedroom, to adorning national book tours, winning awards, and being interviewed by magazines, radio stations, and newspapers. Not to mention, selling hundreds of thousands of books independently. Let's be clear, I didn't go to college to become a writer. I've never majored in Journalism/Arts & Humanities or any other writing major. In fact, being a writer was never even a part of my plan. It was my very own personal story that inspired me to write my first book. Now clearly, I knew that the title of my first book, "A Hood Chick's Story" was bold and colorful; and, that I was taking a risk by using it. That risk was possibly being pigeon-holed into one genre and not achieving commercial success because I was embarking on a journey into a genre that was only semi-popular and somewhat undermined at the time. A genre called, urban fiction. Luckily for me, that didn't happen!

I didn't sign with a large or a small publishing company, nor did I get a sign-on bonus to help jumpstart my career. In fact, my budget was extremely limited at the time. The credit for my success would have to go to adhering to a plan that I thoroughly crafted for myself. Research was my best friend. I read any and everything about self-publishing, how to secure distribution deals, and what helped Authors before me become successful. I literally didn't sleep for months as I digested all the information the internet and library offered for me to consume. Unfortunately, I didn't have a book like this for reference, and I can't begin to tell you about all of the rude replies I received from some of the veteran Authors I reached out to for guidance. It was devastating, but I didn't let them, or all of the other roadblocks I've encountered along the way deter me from seeing the bigger picture. Endless days and nights were spent studying the industry and creating a marketing lane of my own, and it wasn't easy.

Don't get it twisted, I had to put my hand in plenty of fires and get burned a number of times before I discovered what really worked in publishing. Now, here I am, in a position to be able to share secrets of my publishing success with you. Who would have ever thought that I would go on to write thirteen Best Selling books, sell hundreds of thousands of copies and own my own publishing company? … Just think, it was that same book with the bold and colorful title that ended up being the book that changed my life…

No matter what genre you choose to write in, you have a book inside you that can change your life too! I'm going to show you not only how to write a Best Selling novel, but also how to sell it, how to succeed in the writing industry and how to make that money!

‖ Chapter 1

My Journey

My journey diving into writing, in a professional capacity, started in 2007. At the time, I was in a really dark place. Throughout the years, I had lost a slew of family and friends to death or prison, and the urban community where I grew up was really suffering. One of the first deaths to really hit close to home was when my first love was murdered when I was eighteen years old. I was completely devastated! Even as a writer, I still can't begin to find the right language, words, or expressions to describe my emotions after such a treacherous blow. This was someone that I had shared my heart and my whole world with, and just like that, on Christmas Eve, he was gone. What hurt even more, was that his funeral was held on my birthday, December 29th. I came home on that cold night and sunk into the couch, blankly staring out into the air. Tears cascaded down my face as I digested my loss, as my reality and my tender young heart hurt so badly. My entire world was shaken, and it felt like all of the air in the room was collected inside of my chest. I remember vividly how my little brother used to go out of his way to comfort me. When he saw me cry, he'd rub my back and check to see if I was okay. I'd fight through my tears and smile at him to assure him that I was okay because I could see the sincerity in his young eyes. But in reality, I was far from okay.

Eventually, I isolated myself from people that I loved because I was unaware of how to grieve. I didn't talk to anyone about the way that I felt, and I'd only shed tears privately because I didn't want anyone feeling sorry for me. The best way I knew how to handle my emotions was by picking up my pen. I'd write poems to my first love when I missed him, and without realizing, it was helping me heal. Finally, I was learning how to cope, but it didn't last long. A few years later, I lost my little brother to the same fate; he was murdered. Once again, the world had been ripped from underneath my feet. I felt myself existing, but things didn't seem real. It was as if I was trapped inside of a nightmare that I could never wake myself up from. I didn't understand what I did to deserve these hard losses, and my thought process was in disarray. *How could this happen? How could someone really take someone who was so precious to me, away from me? He was my baby brother, he can't be gone, this can't be real, what the f*ck!* All of these questions along with clouds of disbelief swam through my mind daily. I was literally falling apart, but I couldn't allow myself to completely become unhinged because I knew that my mom needed me.

Looking into my mother's fragile brown eyes, I watched as her soul left her body when my little brother left us. It was then that I realized she needed me more than I needed myself. Yes, I wanted to faint, pass out, and bawl my eyes out in front of her each and every day; but, I also knew that I had to be her backbone. She had just lost her son, her baby boy, a child that she had given birth to; my sibling. He was only eighteen years young and loved by so many people. He had a heart of gold and was my rock. What also hurt was that my older brother was locked away fulfilling an eight-year bid in the penitentiary, and the prison system wouldn't temporarily release him to attend my younger brother's funeral. I was crushed! I could feel my big brother's pain behind that prison wall, losing control of himself, because I felt the same way on the outside. My brothers and I were like triplets. Growing up, I swear we felt when the other was hurt, that's why I knew my older brother was in pain. The weight of the world was now on my shoulders, and there was no way that I'd let my family deteriorate before my eyes. Besides, I knew that my younger brother wouldn't have wanted our family to fall apart.

I did a lot of praying, tons of self-reflecting, and a lot of crying behind closed doors. People praised me for being strong; but, little did they know, my insides were screaming and feeling yanked from within as if I was being tortured. Grieving properly wasn't even an option for me. I was too worried about being there for my family. You would have never been able to tell just by looking at me how much I was hurting inside because I didn't allow anyone to see me fold. I'd smile and thank everyone for their condolences; but to me, showing my vulnerability or emotion was weak, and I needed all the strength I had left for my family.

Unfortunately, I continued to lose more people that I loved to death or prison and had to overcome obstacles that even the strongest soldier would crumble from. Through it all, I garnered strength that I didn't even know that I had. That's when I knew that GOD didn't put all of this pain in my path in vain. I knew that there were more LaShonda DeVaughn's out there that needed to hear my story. GOD revealed what my purpose was through my pain, and it was up to me to turn my losses into wins. I began writing my first book, "A Hood Chick's Story", in 2007 and it took me about six months to complete it. I put all of my raw emotions into the pages of that book, and I even shed tears while writing it. I wanted my readers to feel all of the pain that I kept bottled up inside, and I had hoped that it would help others who lost loved ones in any capacity, to heal. "A Hood Chick's Story" also covered the love of family, the effects of coming from a broken home, the honest and raw lessons learned from growing up in the "hood", unsatisfying relationships, and most of all, survival.

When I wrote the words "the end" on the last page of my book, I felt liberated! I tilted my head up to the ceiling and smiled because I knew that my baby brother was proud of me. I was so excited to get my story out to the masses because finally, I felt like I was healing inside. My pen had helped me to regurgitate all of the hidden pain I kept trapped within, and use it for the greater good. Unfortunately, I soon had to draw back on my excitement when I realized that I had no clue how I was going to get my book into the hands of readers. That's when I turned to the internet and quickly got on my grind. I researched publishing companies that published books in my genre, and I paid close attention to their submission guidelines. Once I had my manuscript packaged to submit to about ten publishing houses, I knew that I was ready. I sashayed into the post office like a BOSS! I was confident that I'd receive acceptance letters easily. Or so I thought.

Weeks turned to days, and days turned to months, and I didn't hear anything back from any of the publishing companies that I sought after. I found myself checking my mailbox daily hoping that I would get an acceptance letter. Still, I received nothing, not even an email. I was determined not to get discouraged. While my book was in limbo with the various publishing houses, I reached out to veteran Authors from various genres seeking advice. Call it naïve, but I assumed that they'd be delighted to help out a new, hungry, young Author. Unfortunately, it was just the opposite. Some didn't respond at all while others would offer one-liners full of nothing. I told myself that as soon as I learned the game, that I'd purposely use my influence to help up-and-coming Authors. Not sharing your knowledge has always been whack to me and I couldn't wait to learn everything I could.

While waiting, I began to discover the beautiful world of self-publishing and all of its quirky components, and it fascinated me. When I say that I was obsessed with all of the offerings of self-publishing, I felt like a kid in a candy store! I was wholly convinced that this was the route that I wanted to take. I was especially attracted to the fact that I'd be able to control my own vision, brand, and revenue. I connected with being my own boss and I was completely enveloped into bringing that vision to fruition. I was entirely determined to make sure that I wouldn't stop until I executed it. I had done all of my research, created a plan, and now it was time to take my books from my bedroom to the top of the charts.

Finally, the letters from the publishing companies started strolling in once I decided to self-publish. The rejection letters came in first, but I didn't allow them to get me down because I was on a mission. I grew excited about my mission by the day. I had a solid plan set in place to rock the book industry. I trashed the rejection letters and began to put in the footwork to self-publish. I swear it was like instantaneously, publishing houses large and small started contacting me. This time, these weren't rejection letters. Some contacted me via mail, some by email, and then came the phone calls all with hopes of signing me. I was in disbelief, but I was humbled and honored. I was elated because I felt a sense of validation that these publishing companies obviously saw the same vision that I saw in my work, and it wasn't just a mirage. I was offered sign-on bonuses, two-to-four book deals, and offers to buy my book outright. It was so exciting, but I had to think logically. Once again, I channeled my experiences from my environment growing up, and I used my keen business sense to think strategically. I grew up with hustlers, survivors, and people who could essentially sell water to a whale. I've watched people turn a penny into thousands, and I knew that I could do the same. With much thought, it was a hard decision, but I kindly rejected all offers and jumped into self-publishing with a whole heart.

I named my publishing company, "StreetDreamz Publications" before later changing it to LSDV Publications. The name StreetDreamz Publications, to me, paid homage to the streets that raised me and taught me life lessons, ultimately positioning me to be a dreamer. Also, the genre that I was writing in, *Urban Fiction*, is also sometimes referred to as *Street Fiction* or *Street Lit* and I felt like I had one of the best street fiction books that would hit the market!

I was told by many individuals that I was committing career suicide by rejecting the offers from the publishing companies. People didn't understand why I would turn down major companies that could automatically have my books in mainstream stores that were out of my reach. Their doubt only challenged me to prove them wrong. I had this profound story on my hands that needed to be heard. This book was a reflection of me and the beginning of me living in my purpose, which was to reach people through my writing.

I've learned many hard lessons through trial and error in this industry and man let me tell you, I've made some expensive mistakes which I will explain later on in this book. There were lessons that I've learned that had I signed to a publishing company, I would have never been privy to. I'm a firm believer in mastering everything you do, and I was determined to correct all of my mistakes and discover the best approach to win. I'm not saying that I found all the right answers because just as much as there is useful information out on the market, there's also bad information. I've made diabolical mistakes and I've also made great decisions as well. Everything I've learned or lost helped me to now maneuver through the industry with ease because of the knowledge that I've acquired along the way.

Being an Author, especially a self-published Author, is essentially like starting a small business from scratch. You have to learn who your demographic is, market to that demographic, and continue to evolve against your competitors. Taking your brand to the next level should always be your focus. Once I treated my book like a business and a brand, I was able to get more traction. Soon my books were in the same stores that my naysayers doubted that I could get placement in. Magazines began reaching out, newspapers, book clubs, and bloggers. My mind was blown at how fast everything was happening. What made me feel the most accomplished was when all the emails from young men and women strolled in explaining how much they related to my books, and how it was helping them heal. Finally, I was fully walking in my purpose and made it my mission to level up each year.

I really wanted to write this book for Authors years ago, but I'm glad that I waited to do it now, because I wanted to harness my expertise to the max before I offered it to new Authors.

I willingly gave away tons of jewels throughout the years, and I've watched incredible new Authors use what I taught them to soar to the top. I would always beam with joy at their success because I was fulfilling my promise, which was to help new Authors when I learned my way through this game. You don't understand how much I wished I had someone who could help me navigate and unselfishly share what worked for them when I first started out. I yearned for a book mentor, and I'm happy that I can be that for you.

In my early self-publishing days, I'd get emails from many aspiring Authors asking me what I was doing to move my books so fluidly. I would share my knowledge with no qualms. I remember so clearly how my ex-husband would holler and scream in my ear about giving away information for free. However, his opinion didn't resonate with me because I didn't feel that I was at a level in my career, back then, to charge people for the knowledge that I was sharing. Not to mention, I was still learning myself. He told me that I should never give jewels away for free. Needless to say, I didn't listen to him, and there's obvious reasons why he is my "ex-husband", but that's a whole 'nother book (smile). In all fairness, being a boss means that you must mentor new talent even before you become a boss. Some of my most loyal readers have become Authors because I've helped them transition their curiosity of being published into a book. Individuals will always remember who helped them plant their seed and that's what earns you your respect. Always hold your integrity close to your heart. Teaching others and positioning dreamers for success is my specialty. Ten years of publishing knowledge later, here I am, now a certified Literary Expert. I offer literary coaching and in-depth courses with airtight strategies for hungry Authors. Not bad for a girl from the hood with love for the pen, huh? Now it's time to teach you what I know!

‖ Chapter 2

Let's Get Started!

Okay, let's jump right into it because right now, you should be writing, right? Of course you should! No matter if you're flushing out one hundred, or one thousand words per night, you must get into the routine of writing every single day. It takes a lot of hard work, dedication, and discipline but you MUST be able to commit to it. Some of you are reading this right now saying, "I don't have time to write every day." Well, if that's the case, this isn't the book for you. This book is about getting the desired results you are seeking in your literary journey and keeping you focused. I'm completely dedicated to helping those of you who are serious about your craft and need assistance with executing your plan. In these pages, I'm not going to sugarcoat the good, bad, and the ugly truths about the writing industry. I'm also not going to inundate you with boring, obvious information. I'm unveiling my honest experience, but one thing is for sure before I get started, if *writing a book* is your goal, first thing's first, you must WRITE!

Now, let me ask you this. How long have you had that idea for a book in your head? Or maybe writing a book is something that you want to check off your bucket list. Maybe you've toyed with the idea of writing your own life story or even thought about a self-help book offering valuable information to help others. Well, guess what? No one will read an idea shelved in your head. Give the people what they want and flush out that book!

I get tons of emails asking me the same question, "LaShonda, I got this great idea for a book, where should I start?" My answer is always the same. You have to start by writing it first. What good is an idea for a book that remains unwritten? I can't stress that enough. If you believe in your story, start working on it. Once you finish it, you'd be surprised how many other people will believe in your story too. There's a great quote by Lao Tzu that I live by, *"The journey of a thousand miles starts with a single step."* Now let that inspiration sink in for a moment as you prepare to take your first step towards finishing your book.

Determine what you want out of this. Are you embarking on this journey to become a full-time writer? Did you decide if you wanted to self-publish or get signed by a publisher yet? You may even be entertaining the idea of starting your own publishing company later. Or like many new writers, you just want to finish that book that you promised yourself you'd finish. Whichever literary goal that you choose, committing to it is the first step.

Incorporate writing into your daily habits. Maybe you like going to the gym, watching reality show recaps on your lunch break at work, or gossiping on the phone every night about how much you can't stand your co-workers. Think about a habit or hobby that is embedded into your daily routine and replace it or integrate time in between with writing. I know it's hard to replace that late night McDonald's run for writing, but I guarantee you, it will be so worth it! Remember, if you don't commit to spending time writing your story, it will NEVER happen. Procrastination is the biggest dream killer, and we procrastinate out of fear.

If you have made it this far reading through these pages, then I'm excited for you. Congratulations! Welcome to the first step towards your literary career. You should be excited too. This means that you are committed to getting your project done and now it's time to get started.

The goal is to carve 3-6 months out of your life to finish your book. Start by *free-writing*, every day. Free writing is simply writing about anything that comes to your mind. Just allow the words to flow and eventually your words will start to develop a story. The first major key to being a successful writer is developing your story, or as I like to call it; *creating*.

I first discovered my creative chord in High School. I'll never forget my eleventh grade English teacher, Mr. Golden. It seemed as if he had worn the same damn gray suit every single day. I only noticed because I used to stare at him while he drank his coffee. His thick peppered colored mustache was always saturated in more coffee than he actually consumed with each sip. I used to sit across from him in the front row in class, rolling my eyes, banging my yellow number two pencil on my desk, bored to death because he forced us to free-write every morning. At least as a teenager, I felt like I was being forced to, and I wasn't interested. Every morning he would tell us to open our little flat blue journals and free-write about anything that came to mind, and it used to annoy me to no end.

"Open your book and write LaShonda," he'd say while walking toward me, holding out a piece of crumpled white tissue for me to spit out my bubble gum in. I'd then open my book and surrender to free-writing. After a while, I got a little creative with my writing. I would free-write about the boy I had a crush on, the violence that was happening in my neighborhood, or all the catty drama my friends and I were going through at the time. Writing became my therapy, my outlet, my escape. Once I got into the routine of free-writing, it wasn't long before I fell in love with it. Mr. Golden then introduced the class to metaphors and similes and taught us how to use those methods to flush out and develop the

24

stories we were free-writing. He'd give us weekly assignments to challenge our creativity and finally, I was excited about it. I was so intrigued that I began to take writing seriously. I started writing poems outside of class, using the same formula that Mr. Golden taught me in regard to flirting with wordplay. The beauty of how expressive I was becoming with my words and how I was literally creating real stories and poems through pure imagination was brilliant to me.

When I wrote and published my first book, "A Hood Chick's Story", I always kept Mr. Golden in mind. I appreciated how he assisted me with my first real introduction into taking literature seriously. He may never know it but he helped me discover my niche. It was then that literature proposed to me in High School, I broke up with it years later and never really took it seriously. It was after I wrote my first book, "A Hood Chick's Story," that I finally married it.

Don't be discouraged if you've never had a Mr. Golden or never taken a writing class. As I stated before, you don't have to have a degree in writing; in fact, many Authors that I know personally, have degrees in other fields or no degree at all. If you believe in your story, stay disciplined in writing it, and you can create a legendary masterpiece. Also keep in mind that you don't have to be the best speller or a master of grammar to be a writer, that's what editors are for. I've discovered that some Authors are great writers while others are great storytellers. Usually the storytellers are the writers with longevity in this industry because the majority of the time, they have better material.

Okay, back to free-writing. If you are starting with a blank canvas and you're unable to free-write or get at least one word written down because of writer's block, don't get discouraged. You may not be confident just yet and you're allowing your writing insecurities to hold your creativity hostage. If this is your current situation, I suggest starting with writing your synopsis first. More than likely you already know what you want your book to be about and I'm assuming that you know *why* you would like for people to read it. But for some reason you can't get a single alphabet written down because you are stuck. Again, it's that creative block discouraging you from figuring out where to start. This is where your synopsis can act as a tool to force out your ideas.

Creating your synopsis is similar to your book's skeleton or blue print for your story. Once it's created, it can actually enhance your ideas and entice you to begin writing your book. A synopsis is simply an outline of the plot of a book, play, movie, or episode of a television show. In your case, it's the plot or short outline of *your* book. It's also the description you will use as advertisement on the back of your book as well as on any website advertising for you, including your own. You'll also use it on all promotional tools used to promote your book. This is why your synopsis is so important.

In writing your synopsis, the idea is to draw your consumer into wanting to read your work. I suggest you start by coming up with some interesting character names and begin writing the description of your story without giving away too much of your book. For example, below is the synopsis for my book, "If All Men Cheat, All Women Should Too!" Feel free to use it as a reference guide for structuring your own synopsis:

Synopsis:

"Imagine you're a beautiful woman, body like a brick house, career driven, could cook like a Southern chef, clean like a veteran maid and sex your man like a porn star. Now imagine being in a relationship with a man who is unapologetically mentally and verbally abusive, disrespectful, AND cheats on you! That's just a brief description of Janae's relationship with Tae.

Tae was absolutely cocky, he no longer cared about hiding his cheating; he figured, if Janae hadn't left him the first time she found out he was cheating, then she probably wouldn't leave him the next...

27

Most people would dismiss a girl like Janae as stupid and naïve; someone who needed to wake up and realize that there were other men in this world and move on. But when a man has a mental hold on you, for some women, it's not that easy.

Tae robbed Janae of her self-esteem. His constant put-downs and unfiltered disrespect became the norm for her. He frowned at her tears and did as he pleased. His actions forced Janae to compare herself to the women he cheated with and wonder why she wasn't good enough. Eventually, trying to please Tae became her only purpose.

Being a faithful girlfriend was something Janae took pride in. Somehow, she allowed Tae to define her; she felt like she wasn't whole without him. Finally, a series of events helped Janae discover her worth...

Still withering in the wings of her broken relationship, will Janae stay with Tae and believe that he can and will change? Or will she rebel and act upon the old adage, 'if you can't beat em', join em'?"

Notice how I immediately grabbed the reader's attention and swallowed them in within the first sentence. That should always be your approach. I gave a description of the main character, what she's going through and then I went right into the thick of her relationship and the dilemmas she's facing without giving too much away. Also, notice how I *ended* my synopsis with a question. I use this formula to keep my readers intrigued. You want your reader's mouths watering and craving to explore the pages of the inside of your book. You can use this same formula for any genre including nonfiction books.

When it comes to nonfiction, remember your book is based upon facts. Therefore, you must reel your readers in by making them believe in your story, expertise or the information you are selling. If it's a "self-help" or "how-to" book, make sure your credentials are explained somewhere within your content and give clear examples of why a reader could learn from your knowledge. If your purpose is to touch or impact lives, we must see examples of what qualifies you to teach so that your content is deemed believable.

A great nonfiction book's synopsis example is Steve Harvey's book, "Act Like A Woman, Think Like A Man". When you get a chance, go take a look at how his synopsis is formatted on platforms such as Amazon and Barnes and Noble. Steve's synopsis is thorough and informative. It explains what his book is about and also lists key points that include interesting topics to peak a consumer's interest. He cleverly lists these points in his synopsis with the intent to draw the reader in with clear examples of how well versed he is on the subject matter he is selling which is relationships. Also, notice how before and after his synopsis, he included blurbs from other Authors and magazines.

Soooo...Let me quickly explain what blurbs are...

Blurbs are great for both fiction and nonfiction books. They are simply praises from someone or a group of individuals who have already read and enjoyed your book. Namely, book clubs, magazines, reporters, etc. Don't feel pressured into believing that you need blurbs from the *higher-ups* like magazine's, reporters, etc., in order to feel validated. True, they are great to have, but they are not needed.

Let me let you in on a secret that I used in the beginning of my career. The protocol for gathering blurbs is to send a few pre-chapters or even your entire manuscript to book clubs, Best Selling Authors, magazines, reporters etc. You ask them to read and review your chapters and write you a credible blurb so that you can place it on your book. Now reference back to earlier when I told you that I was going to share some of the good, bad and the ugly about this industry. Well this is where I must reveal one of the ugly truths.

You ready? Okay, many of the Authors and book clubs that you will be sending your book to, will never return your email or your social media inbox requests for a blurb because *they don't know you*. And if your book is written in their genre, they may even view you as competition. Sounds whack right? Well, it's the nature of the game. Another ugly truth is that many Authors or organizations won't take you seriously as a fixture in the industry until you make a name for yourself. But relax, because it's okay! Even with that in mind, you should still be jumping into this industry with the mindset of knowing with assured confidence that you will excel to the level of your peers or higher one day. With that being said, let me get back to my secret on this subject.

Collect blurbs from friends or family members. You heard me right! If they've enjoyed your book, have them write a short blurb and place that baby smack dab on your book cover, the first page of your book or on your back cover. Whichever marketing zone you choose to have this praise for your work to be shown, place it there. I used to have my blurbs placed on the front covers of all of my books. Please believe, blurbs from family members or friends will most likely have the same impact as it would if they were blurbs from a professor or reporter.

If Lana Jones is your mom and she read your book and enjoyed it, let her write you a blurb. List that blurb on your book with no regret. That's your stamp of approval. Especially if you've sent your manuscript to other Authors or book clubs and you're torturing yourself by twiddling your thumbs and biting your nails, awaiting a blurb you may never receive. No way! In this industry, you don't have any time to waste on trivial components like waiting for a blurb. The show must go on. List that blurb from your mom or from a friend that enjoyed your story and be proud of it. As you build your brand and find your way in this industry, things like getting a blurb from someone you respect, will be a breeze.

Your blurb does not need to be a full paragraph either. One-to-three sentences is usually the norm. Below is an example of a blurb you can use for reference:

-After reading this book, I've learned exactly where to find resources to help take my business to the next level. I'm confident that the revenue for my company will triple after applying the techniques I've learned from reading this gem. An absolute masterpiece, every new business owner should read this book!

-Lana Jones

See how easy that was. No one knows that Lana Jones is your mom. As far as they are concerned, she's someone important who read and learned from your book. Also, be sure not to over-do it. You don't need too many blurbs on your book cover, save the others for your website. Some Authors choose not to use blurbs on their book covers at all, they only list them on their websites or on social media. As your name grows and your platform expands, you'll start receiving official blurbs from some of the people you wished would have contacted you when you reached out. I'll let you decide if you still want a blurb from these resources after they made you wait. Wink* Wink* lol….

As I stated, once you generate momentum, getting blurbs will be the least of your worries, but in the beginning of your career, unless you are an expert and already receive blurbs on articles you've written or you're a speaker and you receive blurbs at that capacity, it's a tad bit harder for a newbie. In some respects, your peers feel as though you must prove yourself before they can validate your work, even if they've loved the chapters you sent them. Don't take it personal and I hope none of you hop into anyone's inbox to curse them out for not responding back to you timely, lol. The wait could be nerve plucking, especially when you want to get your cover generated with a blurb on it and waiting for the blurb you were promised, holds you up. Take it with a grain of salt, this is a business and should be treated as such. You don't want to make enemies in this industry. Every relationship rather you feel it is solid or not, should be used as leverage as you grow and expand.

‖Chapter 3

Outline

If you have done any research in the past about how to write a book, I'm sure you've encountered various experts speaking about creating an outline. I definitely recommend an outline to help catapult you out of your writing rut and keep you organized while developing your story. Outlines usually cover the description of your characters, the direction and development of the beginning, plot, climax and ending of your story. The outline method works for many Authors. As for me, well I'm a scattered writer. Nine times out of ten, my ending is usually written before I even begin writing the beginning of my book. I may go back and edit the ending accordingly, but I usually always know how I want my book to end. By doing this, it helps me to stay focused on the direction that my plot development should be heading in and it's just easier for me to carve my writing toward an already developed ending.

Please note, I didn't reference *my* method of writing to confuse you. That's just my personal flow. Don't waste time wondering if you are a scattered writer or an outline writer; your method will develop naturally. Many writers don't feel the need to use an outline at all or any form of a writing GPS or map to navigate through their stories; they just write. I want you to do the same. Allow your process to emerge organically. Your own methods will produce better results anyway, and you will quickly learn what that method is. As you begin to write, you will find a writing scheme that caters to your style and it will bring out your inner greatness and you will finish strong.

So far, in reading this, I hope that you started working on your book on your free time. Hopefully you were able to write your synopsis and it sparked excitement about your story development and in turn, you started crafting something juicy. I have hopes that by now, you are a few chapters or so in. If so, great, that's progress! As writers, once you find your rhythm, it's best to try to keep that momentum going because trust me, it's really easy to get distracted and push your manuscript aside. Hitting those creative stumbling blocks can really be detrimental to your execution.

If free-writing or writing your synopsis didn't bring out any inspiration to write, then trying out an outline may be beneficial. I'll give an example of how to craft an outline in a second but first I want to introduce another form of an outline that may be useful for you; a *visual* outline! Many writers enjoy the process of cutting out pictures of celebrities, every day people or images of locations from magazines or printing out online ads. They take these photos and pin them up on a vision board and visualize their story in color. Try playing with this option and see if it brings out your creativity. You never know, you may discover that you are more of a visual writer and your creativity may flow taking that route. If not, general outlining may be your lane. Outlines are simple so you definitely don't have to take too much time formatting one. Leave all of the formal formatting of your manuscript to your editors once your book is done. At the outline stage, your main concern should be focusing on finishing your book.

Below is a simple way you can start on an outline so that hopefully your bullet points will urge you to start making your story come together. I recommend numbering and titling your chapters in your outline. The titles themselves should encourage you to want to write.

Below I listed a short example of a **Non-Fiction** outline:

- *(Non-Fiction Outline- 2 Chapter example)*

Sample Book Title: How to Love yourself

Chapter 1 – Loving Yourself

- Dive into reasons why loving yourself is important. List examples of self-love and exercises on how to increase self-care.

- Give examples of what worked for me when I was in my darkest place. Explain how I became an expert in self-awareness and how loving who you are internally first, is key.
- I will end this chapter with spelling out reasons why loving yourself can lead to a healthier life.

Chapter 2 – Enjoying Life

- List reasons why ideas like traveling abroad can help individuals appreciate nature and all of earth's offerings.
- Insert my experience traveling to China and how it helped me appreciate life and how I garnered a different prospective relating to fostering relationships with strangers.

See how easy that was. Don't overthink it. You can make your outline as simple or as complex as you need to. Feel free to list as many bullet points as you desire to help curate the perfect chapter content. And you don't always have to list long sentences. Beside some of your bullet points, single word descriptions can be used to help you generalize where to insert certain characters or descriptions. As long as it's enough to spark content for that particular chapter.

Below is a two-chapter sample of a **Fictional** outline. Same rules apply as above. Some of your bullet points can be short and concise but should help aim you in the direction of how you want your chapter formatted.

- *(2 Chapter, Fiction Outline)*

Sample Book Title: Sheila's Fate

Chapter 1 – Sheila's introduction

- Introduce Sheila. Describe her body shape, her personality, the way she talks and walks everywhere, wearing out the soles of all of her shoes because she doesn't have a car. Go deep into her backstory, reveal why she's insecure and why she's giving up on her dream to finish College.
- Describe why Sheila's getting fired from her job and why she's being evicted from her home.
- Introduce Sheila's mom and create dialogue between the two characters concerning how Sheila's forced to move back in with her mom in Atlanta since she's lost everything in Charlotte. Make sure the dialogue is intense between the two, by bringing up the family's secret about Sheila's childhood abuse but don't give away who actually abused her in this chapter.

Chapter 2 – The Family Secret

- Introduce Sheila's grandmother and step-dad who also lives with Sheila's mom. Describe her disdain for moving back in with them. Explain why she has an estranged relationship with these family members.
- Sheila's emotionally unavailable grandmother will start conflict with Sheila right away and her step-dad who despises Sheila's grandmother and his own wife will jump in to defend Sheila. Since Atlanta is Sheila's new residency, I will need to research

places in Atlanta where Sheila's mom can introduce a family reunion announcement.

- End this chapter with the family heading to the reunion. Introduce her abusive cousin Marko. Have him appear drunk entering the family reunion while everyone looks upon him with disgust. Tell his backstory. Describe how he was also abused as a child and why abuse is now a generational curse in their family.

Boom! There's your example of an outline for a fiction book. Magically, your bullet points should guide you with ease to write through your chapters for both a fiction and a nonfiction book. As you use your outline as your navigation, you will naturally start to develop your story and you will actually start to feel like a writer (smile). Also, cross out each bullet point after using the content so that you know that you are on track. This will also help you to feel encouraged because as you cross out each line, you will realize that you are making progress.

Now that you know what an outline is and how easy it is to create one, you're now on your way! I'm hopeful that by trying out one of these techniques, you'll be encourage to write your tail off and enjoy the journey along the way. Writing your book should be fun, it shouldn't feel like a dreadful assignment or task. So enjoy every step!

Trust me, I know that writing and completing a book is a process, but the process isn't as difficult as it seems. It's actually quite simple once you get started and stay focused. If writer's block continues to cage in your creativity, don't fret, there are plenty of techniques to help unlock your creative juices. I'm not only going to present these techniques but also show you how to apply them.

‖ Chapter 4

Writer's Block

Writer's Block is every writer's worst nightmare. And unfortunately, it happens to the best of us. I remember posting on social media that I had a bad case of writer's block one night and immediately I received instant messages from aspiring Authors asking, "wow, you get writer's block too"? The answer to that question is, absolutely! Even the most successful writers experience writer's block. Unfortunately, no one is exempt from the throws of hitting a creative stumbling block. The good news is, I've developed strategies to help combat writer's block. Over the years, these techniques have worked for me and I encourage you to try them when you find yourself unable to create content.

The beauty of overcoming writer's block is that once you are able to get in your zone, words pour from you and mysterious depths of creativity arise suddenly. Each and every one of our methods of writing vary. Even the places that we choose to write in vary. You may find yourself in a café, writing by the water, in a quiet place or writing while listening to music or in total isolation. You literally have to find your own rhythm. For me, there are times where I need to write at home alone in my room with the television and music turned off. Sometimes I need to write in my office with the window open so that I can hear the calms of nature. Other times I like to write with all of the chaos, noise and mayhem going on in my house. And although I tune out the noise, somehow it helps with my flow. It all depends on my mood.

One of the best methods to combat writer's block is to write when you feel inspired. When you neglect that chance to ignite some great content, you later find yourself wishing that you wrote down your thoughts. Try not to dampen your urge to write. Whenever you feel the need to add a great addition to your story, jot it down or record it so that you can add it to your manuscript later. Never let a chance of adding to your story get away from you because you will find yourself regretting it later.

Now let's talk about some of the other methods that you can practice to tackle writer's block head on. What I like to do to open up new areas of creativity is to listen to music outside of the genre that I normally listen to. My friends and family know that I love me some Hip-Hop and R&B music, but when I'm trying to create, it only distracts me. So I'll search for a Country or Rock song with deep lyrics and let the inspiration flow. Trust me, this method has done wonders for me. It has helped me develop characters that

I felt needed more depth and was also great in helping me expand on my love scenes.

Another very productive method of fighting through your creative stump is by simply stepping away from your work. I can't begin to tell you how many times I shut down my computer to go make myself a meal, only to return to my work and create more content. It gives you time to step away from your work, recharge and revisit it with a different mindset.

Watching a movie outside of your typical movie taste works as well. Try watching an old black and white flick from the 50's or 60's. The depth of the movies during that time is so inspiring; you're liable to crack open your laptop and pull an all-nighter. Sounds comical but it's true. Watching a movie outside of my normal genre, has helped ignite my creative flame on plenty of occasions. Another great method of beating writer's block is to take a ride in your car with no music on at all. Allow your characters and scenes to speak to you. Sit with your own thoughts and allow fresh material to find its way to your story. Even taking long walks alone and observing nature can help spark your creativity. It doesn't take much for a writer to be inspired.

Setting deadlines is also a great method. But be sure to set realistic expectations on yourself. If you work full-time, have a family at home and have to bring your kids to practice for sports and or to tutors, don't set a 2-day, 20k word count goal. Give yourself time to meet your deadline. Set the date on your calendar and stick to your goal. A realistic goal is giving yourself 7 days to achieve a 10-15k word count goal or 3-6 months to finish a book completely. If you hold yourself accountable, you can achieve your writing goals and it can also push you through writer's block because you are aware that you have a goal to meet. Setting deadlines can give you a surge of confidence because you are under pressure to finish a goal that you are holding yourself accountable for.

The best advice that I can give on writer's block is to not let it lead you, you have to lead it. When you find yourself unable to create, try one of my suggested methods. Shutting down your laptop and putting your writing off for the next day is the worst type of procrastination for a writer. You must push through. Believe in yourself because you can do it! There are days when writing seems impossible but you must sacrifice and get it done. Your goal is to become a writer, correct? Well until you are able to finish your manuscript, dreams of becoming a writer are just those, dreams. You want to make your dreams a reality. A reality that is beneficial and profitable.

‖ Chapter 5

The 3 Phases of Writing

Introducing... The Three Phases Of Writing

Listen closely because these steps are critical in helping with the development of birthing your book. The three phases of writing are simply, the **story phase**, the **title phase** and the **ending**. Making sure you address all three of these phases separately (and not in any particular order) is what's going to keep you on track to creating the perfect formula for a best-selling book.

We've already talked a little bit about the story phase, which is *writing* it and we'll revisit the writing phase again in a moment. Now let's talk a little bit about the **TITLE** phase. Some of you have already had your title handpicked even before you've written anything down. Others like to conjure up a title after they've finished writing their book because their story sometimes heads in a total different direction than they had initially anticipated. Either way, you must keep in mind that your title is what attracts a consumer to your book. The title is even more important than your book *cover art*. An Author can have the most beautiful work of art dressed on the front of their book but if you are a new Author, and your name isn't Steven Spielberg, chances are, readers may be hesitant to put their trust into knowing if your book is a book that they may enjoy. So what's going to make them want to take a peek inside your book in the first place? That's right, your TITLE! Not your cover art (although this is important too).

If your TITLE sounds interesting and enticing, the first thing a reader will do is turn over your book to read your synopsis. Or they may open up the first page of your book to see if they are still interested after judging your intro and writing style. You get it now? Your title is what made them pick up your book in the first place. Your title is vital to your writing success because it's essentially your general sales pitch and your synopsis or first page of your book is how you close the sale.

Your title should be catchy, relevant and exude that "wow" factor. Here's a selling secret into choosing the perfect title. You ready? Okay, first you must decide what genre you are writing in. Are you writing a how-to book, a biography, autobiography (nonfiction) or are you writing a story that you created through your imagination and brainstorming (fiction)? Once you have that figured out, the secret is to study all of the Authors that are currently thriving in your genre on the Best Sellers Lists.

Put your genre in the search filter and take a close look at the Amazon and Barnes and Noble Best Selling charts and study the titles that are in the top 20 in the same genre that you plan to write in. You may see a common theme or trend within the book cover titles. This is when you can get creative with coming up with a title that would work best for you. For example, on the Amazon Best Selling chart for Romance, say the top three titles are "Love, Sex and Passion", "Loving him with Passion" and "The Passion of Love". Do you see the common theme here? The words **Love** and **Passion** are repeated which means that these are keywords that are being recognized by the community of the e-reader system, the Amazon Algorithm.

The Amazon Algorithm is a code to help Amazon sort and load product lists for their customer's satisfying experiences. By placing one or both of these words in your title can help your book become recognized amongst the top reads because of other customers who purchased similar titles. Sounds easy right? Well if done correctly, it can really land you success in competing for a top spot. Your title will be more visual because it'll be recommended by the selling platform as a book to read all because you were strategic with your titling.

Choosing your book title is actually one of the hardest parts of publishing a book because sometimes it can make or break you. However, by using the secret I just revealed, you can be off to a great start and began generating a ton of income once your book is circulating with your competitors. Your strategy will attract their built in readership.

New writers often have a hard time creating an audience because of their title. We all want our title to be unique and most aspiring Authors already had a title handpicked for as long as the book idea existed. Well guess what? If your goal is to make money and build an audience, you must be strategic, not hasty. By no means am I trying to dismantle your title; what I *am* doing is teaching you how to sell your book and profit from it.

Remember, your book may be better than many of the veteran Authors on the top 20 Best Seller's lists but if you choose to title your book a non-competitive title, you may not get the proper visibility online. I'm not saying nix your entire title idea, but I do encourage you to add in a key word(s) in your title to compete with the books ranked high on the charts. This will enable your book to be recognized as a title of interest.

Alright, now that you have an idea of how to create a title to catch your reader's attention, it's time to really sell them on your product so that they will become returning customers. They've already liked your title, now they must *LOVE* your story.

Now let's revisit writing and the creation of your manuscript, which again is the **story phase**. A phase you will constantly revisit after finding yourself re-writing and re-editing your work over and over again until you feel that it's at its best. I sincerely encourage you to try to avoid re-writing your story continuously. You will spend lots of wasted time rewriting and critiquing your own work when you should really be focusing on finishing your book. Trust me, I used to find myself writing three chapters of a new book and then going back and re-reading it and re-writing the same paragraphs over again for months at a time. What I should have been doing was finishing my book to its entirety and re-writing it and editing myself later. I call this the *Rewind Game*. Don't get caught up on rewinding when you should be pressing forward with your story. The more progress towards finishing your book, the better. As you get excited about writing your story, your creative juices will take over effortlessly!

The moment that you'll really start to feel like a writer is when you find yourself in random places with an urge to write bits and pieces of your story down. That's when you'll pull out your phone, take small pieces of scrap paper out of your purse or back pocket to write down your ideas. Or, if you're like me, you will pull over your car to write ideas down on napkins that you find on the floor of your vehicle. Yes, this actually happens to me all the time! Inspiration can literally come from anywhere, at any time. And usually, the most random ideas are some of the most intricate additions to your story. You'll really start to feel like a writer for real!

Now translating those random pieces of your story from your scrap paper and placing them into context or into your outline is key. Read other books in your genre and be aggressive about thinking outside the box and making your story more compelling than any other book on the market in your genre. That should be your front-lining thoughts as you write. You should be coming for blood. Not literally, but as in any industry, you must be competitive and think big. Write a classic. Your first page should immediately make your consumer want to read more.

My approach to writing is to always ensure that my opening dialogue is addictive and movie-like. If your reader can picture what they are reading from page one, more than likely, they'll want to keep reading and make the purchase. As a writer, this is our job; to attract consumers. You must disrobe your creativity. Especially if you are a new Author, I can't stress this enough. Drawing in your reader as soon as possible is vital and keeping that same momentum throughout your story is essential. This method has been my formula since the beginning of my career. Hold yourself accountable and challenge yourself to add content to your book that reads like a 3-D movie.

You must surrender pieces of yourself into your story. Submit your witt, humor, creativity, and be descriptive. Make sure your reader is getting more than they've bargained for. Offer them a detailed experience, similar to an HD movie, not just a book to read. And your ending should be just as profound as the beginning of your story. When artists write songs, they want you to dance to their lyrics and vibe with the melodies of their beats. Well when you write a book, you want readers to visualize your story as if they're watching a movie in their minds. Telling a story is taking a journey on a path that is expressive. Some of the things that happen to your characters, you wouldn't wish on your worst enemy. But you must trust in your imagination and allow your characters to speak to you so that they can speak to your readers.

Think of your favorite movie. It's your favorite movie because most likely you have a favorite character or characters that attracted your attention and held your interest until the very end. The ending of the movie is usually what makes the movie the most memorable. It's also the reason it became your favorite movie. Your story should be written the same way. You must create memorable characters, dialogue, and create a lasting effect to make readers crave more of your work. If your character is meant to be hated, make sure that you use descriptive words and situations to make your readers face turn up and bodies squirm while reading your story. If one of your characters are meant to be loved, make your reader's hearts melt and fall in love with your character as if they were in a relationship with them themselves.

My secret is to always tap into your reader's emotions. I can't begin to tell you how elevating it is to receive reviews such as these:

"LaShonda, you made me cry again. Tiara went through so much, I wish I could hug her." -Reviewer

"I hated the way Tae made Janae feel, I wanted to jump through the pages and defend her myself." - Reviewer

Reviews like these reassures me that I've done my job. Real and raw emotions should be evoked out of your reader's feelings. If your character is supposed to be lusted after, be sure that you describe your character's personality to be so irresistible that your readers want to date them. If your character should be respected, add in some accolades to make your readers want to hold them at a high regard. Cater your writing towards wanting a reader to want to thank you as the Author for giving them such a grand experience.

Use descriptive words and ensure that your dialogue between your characters are genuine and not forced. For example, I'm sure most of you have seen classic movies such as *The Notebook* or *The Titanic*. Think back on how the characters in the movie forced you to connect with the storyline because of the heartfelt dialogue and chemistry amongst the characters. The screen writers purposely placed the actors in positions so that you as the viewer could bond and connect with them and root for their relationships. You have to get inside your readers headspace the same way. This is the approach you must use when creating your characters. In other words, you have to make your colors come to life, smells bounce off the pages and emotions connect. If you are trying to produce a memorable character, throw in a fancy characteristic or obsession.

For instance, you may want your readers to connect with your character named, *Lea* but you're having a hard time making her a memorable character. Using flowery and colorful words will help to paint the visual of Lea to your readers.

Here's an example: *"Lea wore a red dress that made a ripe strawberry in an all-white room seem dull in comparison. Her red lipstick danced off her face almost in 3-D as she mouthed the words, 'I love you.' I felt her words melt into my heart as it did the first day she expressed her love for me. Lea always wore red, that's why the very thought of her reminded me of the beauty and perfection of the brightest rose."*

See what I did? I didn't just give a general description of Lea. I could have easily just wrote: "Lea wore a red dress and red lipstick to match. Lea loved wearing red." But because we want Lea to be remembered, I used the color red to attach to Lea's character so that you'll always have that visual in your mind when you think of her. I used descriptive words to make the colors come to life and the connection to Lea's lover seem more believable and in turn, you readers will connect with the character too. Trust me, your readers will appreciate you for painting your story in their minds. Allow your characters to express themselves exactly how you see and hear them expressing themselves in your head. Let your characters shine and speak to your readers so that they won't be able to put your book down. And when you give them a mind blowing story, you have to hit a home run with your ending.

When mentoring Authors, I always encourage them to make sure that when someone reads the end of their story, they must walk away thinking about their book long after they are done. I instruct my students to make their characters interesting and relatable by making them seem real. A reader should feel like they know your characters personally. In addition to character development, your plot should be phenomenal and your ending, mind-blowing. Which now brings us to the **Ending Phase**.

The ending of your story is a super important component because it can make or break your story. If you are writing a series and desire to leave a cliffhanger, make sure it's not abrupt; you can easily turn a great book into a bad book.

Here's an example of an abrupt ending/cliffhanger: *"Lea opened the door, she couldn't believe who was standing on the other side of the threshold."* THE END. This ending was abrupt, cut short and didn't provide enough meat to get your reader full. Although your reader may know who's standing on the other side of the threshold, you want to be sure that your consumer is full, yet hungry enough to want a second helping of your story.

Here's an example of an ending that satisfies your reader's appetite:

"Lea opened the door, standing on the other side of the threshold was the love of her life. Her heart sank into her shoes in slow motion and butterflies burst in her gut. Although she missed him, she hated him for taking her through years of emotional turmoil. Her mind was still withering with the decision of taking him back. She widened the door to let him in.

"Jarell, you and I need to talk."

Jarell paused where he stood, took a deep breath and bent down on one knee,

"Lea will you marry me?" He asked.

Lea's heart was stuck in her chest and a teardrop melted out of her right eye. "I can't." She cried.

Lea and Jarell, A Love Story Pt. 2, COMING SOON….

This time, the Author didn't cut the reader short. The Author unmasked who was at the door, then alluded to the fact that a conversation needed to be had. The emotions of the characters were pulled to the forefront and the desires of your readers were met. Your reader now knows who was at the door and why. The anticipation of what Lea will do next is what's going to make your readers want to read part two as well as leave you a review stating this. I can't stress enough how dire your ending phase is to your reputation.

We tend to spend months or even years working on our books and as soon as we hit the finish line, the ease to rush our ending feels tempting just to feel like you've completed your book. Be sure that all questions are answered and all loose ends are tied up before closing out your book. That way, you'll avoid readers asking about unanswered questions in the review section and possibly leaving you an unfavorable review because of this. Avoid rushing! The ending of your book is detrimental to your success. Please avoid making the mistake of rushing your ending and wasting away all of your hard work just to lose readers instead of gaining them because of how you closed out your book.

‖ Chapter 6

Title Pages

Congrats! You now understand the three phases of writing. By now, your **Title**, **Story** and **Ending** should be thoroughly crafted together, you've pushed through writer's block and formatted your manuscript into a story that will blow readers away! If you are *self-publishing*, this will be the time that you would insert your *title page, copyright page, table of contents (this page is optional and mainly used for nonfiction books)* and your *acknowledgement's page*.

All of these pages can be created with ease and used for every book that you publish. I save my *title pages* to my computer and each time I write a book, I update the pages with the current book information and I insert it into my new book. Your copyright page normally stays the same, the year you are publishing your book may be the only portion that you change in this document but your title page and acknowledgements page should always be updated with your new title and new acknowledgment information.

The *title page* for a fiction book should simply consist of your logo (if you have one), the title of your book and the writer/writers that authored the book. Your font can be as fancy or as simple as you'd like. If you are writing a nonfiction book, your title page will consist of the same content minus your logo. Below is a sample of what your title page should look like when a reader opens your book:

LSDV Productions Presents:

Live, Love, Laugh... A Romance Novella

By: LaShonda DeVaughn

Simple, right? This is all that your title page should consist of. It should be clean and professional.

The page after your title page is your *copyright's page*. According to Wikipedia, your copyright notice informs the public that a work is protected by copyright. It identifies the copyright owner, and shows the year of the first publication. Furthermore, in the event that a work is infringed, if the work carries a proper notice, the court will not give any weight to a defendant's use of an innocent infringement defense. In other words, a copyrights page is a disclaimer stating that your work and its content is protected so you won't get sued. Below is an example of a copyright page that I've used inside of my published fiction works:

That's it! Simple and easy. A question some of you are probably wanting to ask right now is, "okay, I see that this is a copyrights page, now how do I get my book copy written?" You ready for the answer? Here's what my Attorney told me. He stated that when you enter a copyright page into your book and seal it with this symbol, "©" (view in the copyright page sample), your book is copy written. Lol, that's it! No, you don't have to do any fancy footwork. Seal your book with the copyright symbol and when you publish it, it's copy written under your name/brand. I'll get into other ways on how to register your book inside book databases such as Bowker later but as far as copywriting your work, per my Attorney, that's all that you have to do my friend.

For nonfiction books, this next page will be used for your *Table Of Contents*. You can spell it out that way or shorten this page to simply *Contents*. The format of your Table Of Contents can be as formal or informal as you desire. Here are two examples:

Table Of Contents - Example: 1

Table Of Contents

Chapter 1: Roses and Thorns...1

Chapter 2: Loving and Hating..12

Table Of Contents - Example: 2

Contents

That's it! Don't waste too much time creating your title pages because there really isn't much to them. As I stated before, keep the format of these pages saved to your computer as your "title pages" and make changes to them accordingly to coincide with each new book that you publish.

Moving on to your acknowledgement's page. This page is very simple but it's also an important addition to your book. It affords you the opportunity to thank those who have supported you and also allows you to reveal a message about why you felt compelled to write your book. This page also exposes a little piece of your personality to your readers so here's your chance to be a bit witty.

In regards to the formation of this page, you can insert your acknowledgement's page in the beginning or end of your book. The choice is yours. The order sequence upon opening a fiction book is normally the title page first, copyright page next and then your acknowledgements page (if you choose to put this page in the beginning). For nonfiction books, the order is usually the title page first and then the copyright page followed by the table of contents. Some nonfiction writers choose not to use an acknowledgements page at all, but that choice is completely up to you.

Here's an example of an Acknowledgements page:

Acknowledgements

First I'd like to thank GOD for the gift of writing. Secondly I'd like to thank my family for supporting me throughout my writing journey. I felt compelled to write this novel to encourage women to travel, experience different cultures, and fall in love with their femininity. I hope that my story can teach you self-love and the importance of self-confidence. Cheers to us ladies, we rock!

-Jane Doe

Your acknowledgements page is basically your "shout-outs" page. I recommend keeping your acknowledgments 1-2 pages in length, no more. Aside from your acknowledgements page, you can also create a dedication page but this is optional. I personally place a dedication page in all of my work because I choose to dedicate all of my books to my late younger brother Andre Stone. It makes me feel as if I'm taking him on this writing journey with me. That's what the beauty of self-publishing does for me. It gives me the creative freedom of creating some of my own rules. Which leads us into the next chapter because you have a decision to make.

‖ Chapter 7

The Decision

Now that your title pages are created, it's time for you to make a decision. The answer to this decision will actually answer if you would even need your title pages. You ready? You must think long and hard on this decision. The question is, do you want to self-publish or get signed to a publishing house? If your plan is to be signed to a publishing house, your publisher will create your title pages for you so you can ditch them if you created them. Use them only if you are self-publishing.

Now about your decision. Think back on my story when I explained how I was faced to decide what path I wanted to take in publishing. Resources were limited at the time so self-publishing wasn't even something that I was considering until I researched it. Before that, I sent my manuscript to various publishing houses hoping for a deal. Today, times have changed and self-publishing is becoming more and more attractive to new writers. With so many different ways to publish, market, and brand yourself; self-publishing is definitely a route that you should consider.

In making this decision, ask yourself what you want out of this. Are you writing a book to highlight your expertise, to write your biography/autobiography or turn this into a career? Obviously you can self-publish in any genre you choose to write in but if you want to turn being a writer into a career, then self-publishing is the route that I would recommend.

Before making the decision to self-publish, remember, you must dedicate yourself into becoming your own machine. You have to literally become your own publishing house. That means if you have a full-time job, you have to also work full-time as your own publisher. If you have a family, hobbies that you are dedicated to or if you travel often, you must take all of that into consideration. Finding ways to incorporate your new writing career is going to be a task that you must be able to accomplish by multi-tasking. Acting as your own publisher is not easy and you must be prepared to tackle challenges that your publisher would have to tackle if you were signed.

Acting as your own machine takes a lot of work. I remember putting in hours at my corporate job and sneaking in time to work on my publishing company, on company time, because it seemed as if carving out time for the publishing process at home wasn't enough. I needed to dedicate day-time hours into watering the seeds I was planting. Sometimes it'd feel like there just wasn't enough time in a day for me to get things done. With hard work, a whole lot of hustle and persistence; you can make it happen too.

The dictionary meaning of self-publishing is *to publish a piece of one's work independently and at one's own expense*. That means, not only do you have to dedicate time, but you also have to dedicate yourself financially. Now, that doesn't mean that you have to go broke writing and publishing your book; that just means that you have to invest in yourself. Like I mentioned earlier, I didn't have a ton of money to invest in my career but as I started making money off of my books, I was able to invest it back into myself.

So let's say that your decision is to take the self-publishing route and you've done your research and now you're interested in applying everything you've learned. Well first things first, since your book should now be finished, that's about 40% of the process. Now you must find a great editor to polish your work so that it's grammatically sound and as error free as possible. While your book is being edited, you have to take the initiative to research graphic designers that have designed book covers in your genre.

I remember trying to find a designer to create a cover for my first book, "A Hood Chick's Story". Usually when finding a designer, you give them your vision of what you want your cover to look like and you also send them your synopsis so that they can see the vision in words. Well the designer I chose, had never created a book cover in my genre before. The company kept sending me back covers that probably should have been created for a children's book. I kept getting discouraged as I rejected each draft that I was sent to review.

Back when I started out, it was harder to find designers because social media was so limited and google didn't offer many suggestions. Luckily for you, all you have to do is use the proper hashtag on Instagram and you can find tons of designers to create a cover for your genre. Social media and the google search engines have expanded at such a large capacity that the designers you can find are endless. Also, here's a secret on this subject. I'm sure you follow some of your favorite Authors, right? Well pay attention to when they post up their new book covers. Often times, they shout out their cover designers. Follow their designers on social media, check their prices and boom, you have found your designer!

So now you found a great editor, one who edits books in your genre by using google, social media or some other large search engine platform. You've also located a book cover designer of your choice which by the way, should create a cover designed to compete with other covers in your genre. Now you must find an outlet to distribute your books. Distribution means, to issue your books to be available to the public. Many self-published Authors prefer to *only* publish and distribute their books as e-books to keep costs low, while others enjoy supplying their readers with both e-books as well as printed books.

Referencing back again to when I started out, e-books didn't exist which is why I'll always have a special love for printed books. I often encourage Authors to use both outlets because it's not only wise as a publisher but also from a business standpoint. It's always wise to have several streams of revenue coming in from your product. Thankfully, today we have sites such as Lightning Source and Create Space that not only prints your books but also distributes them.

Before sites like these were discovered, Authors like myself used to have to cross our fingers and pray that we could secure contracts with the top distributors in the world such as Ingram and Baker and Taylor. I had to hustle and negotiate my way into obtaining a contract with these distributors in order to get my books into major bookstores. It took a lot of proving myself but seeing my books on the bookshelves with Authors that were signed to major publishers made it all worth it.

Top notch distributors like Baker and Taylor and Ingram are responsible for getting your books in major online and offline retailers such as Amazon, Barnes and Noble and even libraries. Lots of Authors struggled to get their books into major bookstores because these distributors weren't easy to secure. Today, these distributors are affiliated with the likes of Lightning Source and Create Space so your books are able to be easily be found by your consumers in the databases of libraries and bookstores. If you publish your printed books on Create Space and choose the option to allow Ingram to be one of your distributors, your book can appear in stores if enough of your readers request them at a particular location.

So let's say that your decision is to self-publish and you want to make your book available as an e-book as well as a printed book. Here's the next step for the printing process. In order to have your book printed into paperback form, you must secure an ISBN number. As a publisher, once I turned my publishing company into an LLC, I headed over to Bowker.com to purchase a block of *ten* ISBN (International Standard Book Numbers) numbers to solidify my publishing company as an official business. ISBN numbers are assigned to each book that you print if you want your books to be sold in stores. Once I purchased a block of ten ISBN numbers, this is what made my company an official publishing company in the eyes of the large distributors. This lets distributors like Ingram know that your company is an official business that would need distribution. This is one of the reasons that I was able to score a contract with them. That was back then. Now, as I mentioned, with sites like Create Space and Lightning Source, these resources are able to supply you with ISBN numbers for your books straight from the site.

Times have definitely changed in publishing but I'd have to say it's for the betterment of the industry. Not only can you purchase ISBN numbers from these sites but you can also get distribution with those large distributors that I've mentioned through these sites as well.

All of the ISBN and distribution jargon may sound intimidating to you which is why many Authors choose to only publish e-books. But honestly, with all the new sites that are able to print your books on demand, it's definitely not as hard as it sounds. When I started out, I had to find physical book companies to print my books. And since I was acting as my own publisher, I also had to act as my own warehouse to store my books. I remember I ordered five thousand copies of "A Hood Chick's Story" which were delivered to my garage. Other Authors told me that ordering five thousand copies was a waste of my time, money and space. They told me that I'd be sitting on five thousand books for years because I wouldn't get proper distribution.

Well once I secured the Ingram deal as well as others, I was sending hundreds of books out at a time. I used to proudly load cases of my books out of my car into Fed Ex because distributors were requesting my books faithfully. Today, the beauty of printing books on demand is fantastic. Through sites like Create Space, you no longer have to house your books at home. You can order books as you need them for your book signings, etc. And consumers are able to order your printed books straight from Amazon with Create Space being the distributor.

Getting your books available via e-books is a simple process and it's FREE! When your manuscript is edited and ready to be published, you head over to Amazon, sign in, click on the "self-publish with us" tab and follow the prompts. Be sure that your book cover designer formats your cover to the Amazon dimensions so that you don't have a problem when you try uploading it. Same process to publish your e-books on Barnes and Noble. Head over to Nook Press, create a log in and follow the prompts. Be sure that your manuscript and cover are both formatted correctly so that when you review the proof, you are satisfied with the formatting and you can publish your book immediately.

Setting your books up for printing is a little more complicated but still not a completely tedious process. Before your books are ready to be printed, you must hire a typesetter. I know you are probably thinking, wow, I need a graphic designer for my cover, editor, ISBN number for my books to be printed and now a typesetter. Well yes, you are your own publisher which means that you are in charge of every single publishing element. A typesetter is in charge of formatting your book for print. For instance, if you are using Create Space to print your book, you will be asked to upload the interior of your book which is your manuscript and it must be formatted properly in order for them to accept it. Your cover must also be formatted in the correct dimensions in order for Create Space to be able to package your book for print.

For instance, my covers are always 5.5 x 8.5 in width and length. You must provide these dimensions to your **cover designer** so that they're able to send you the proper formatted cover so that you can upload it easily onto Create Space for print. You also have to let your **typesetter** know these same exact dimensions so that they can send you a pdf document with the correct interior size. Once your cover and interior are both 5x5 x 8x5 and ready for print, upload them to Create Space (or whatever book printing platform you choose to use) and if your designer and typesetter formatted your books correctly, your printer will accept your book and alert you when it's ready to be proofed.

Once you review the proof, check to see if the book is formatted correctly and that there are no errors. If everything looks good, accept your proof online so that your books can officially be ready for print. You should be ecstatic to be holding your proof! Although it's only a proof, this is your baby that you are holding in your hands. This is the very thing that you have been working hard for. You pushed through writer's block and you are now an Author! Sounds like a lot, but it's really not that bad. Soon you will scout out an editor, graphic designer and typesetter that you trust and that you will use often.

Now let's say your decision is to sign with a publishing house. First you must research publishing companies who publish books in your genre. Once you locate them, study their submission guidelines thoroughly. You may find that some of the publishing companies that you are interested in, have strict guidelines. They may request that you send in your manuscript with particular fonts and paragraph structures. Be sure to adhere to their guidelines before submitting. Typically, many small publishers will request your biography, a synopsis of your story, the first three chapters of your book or your full manuscript. It all depends on the publishing company you are submitting to.

Now, if your goal is to secure a deal with some of the major publishing houses like Simon and Schuster or Random House, you must have an agent. And if getting published is your goal, prepare to wait for an answer. Sometimes it can take months for a publisher to get back to you. It's an extremely grueling process but you never know what might happen so keep an open mind. Not everyone will see your vision. Your entire Church might have sung your praises about how great of a writer you are and how much they've enjoyed reading your manuscript but that doesn't mean your story is what a particular publisher is looking for. So don't get discouraged if you receive rejection letter after rejection letter. For most, that makes self-publishing sound even sweeter. Sometimes rejection letters can filter you to carve your own lane and prove to yourself and to others that your story is worth being read.

Again, if you are still gravitating towards being signed to a major publishing company such as powerful machines like Simon and Schuster and Random house, keep in mind that they have strict gatekeepers. They won't even allow your submission to be glimpsed at if it isn't submitted through an agent. To secure an agent, you must do your due diligence and carefully search for literary agencies that accept books in your genre. Then you must submit a query letter along with three chapters of your book to the agents of your choice so that they can review it and potentially shop your books to publishers and find the best deal to get you signed. Query letters are essentially a proposal that is approximately 200-400 words stating that you are seeking representation. You must include a short bio of yourself, the genre you are writing in, your word count, and a description of your book and why you feel you should be represented. Be sure to describe what sets your book apart from other books in your genre. Keep in mind that you can find existing publishing houses that allow unsolicited manuscripts for review without an agent and usually that information is easily accessible online. But if you are still interested in the larger machines, an agent is necessary.

If an agent likes your work, they will request your entire manuscript. After reviewing your manuscript and they're impressed with your work and feel confident in your story, they will sign you to their agency and began the process of pitching your book to publishers to shop for the best deal. Literary agents usually collect about 15 percent commission off of the deal they secure for the author. At one point in my career, I tried this route. Self-publishing was going incredible for me and normally large publishing houses took note of the authors who were making noise independently. I felt that I attained a lot of success self-publishing and if the deal was right, I'd take the opportunity to sign with a major. That way, I could focus on publishing books from authors that I signed under my new company.

So there I was, staring at an email in my inbox from a literary agent that wanted to sign me. I was excited but at the same time, I was reluctant about surrendering my creative freedom over to a publishing house if I were to get signed. Yet I was curious to see if a larger publishing house could take my career to the next level. The literary agent scheduled a call and I was open to hear what she had to say. She briefed me on her background and told me that she would like to present the opportunity for me to sign to that particular literary agency. I can't lie, I thought long and hard about signing, but I figured if she could get me the right deal, I'd sign and focus on making the careers of the Authors that I was signing to my own company, successful. With the notoriety I was receiving, the long hours that I was grinding, a larger machine behind me would only put more fuel in my tank and enlarge my network. I put on my business hat and began to think strategically. The right deal could be big for both myself and my authors. Besides, if my agent could get me a 2-book deal that included a large advance and then for some reason I was unhappy with the deal, it's only two books that I'd be surrendering. I'd take the knowledge and the know-how from the majors with me if it didn't work out. So I decided that I'd sign with the literary agent and see what happens.

It didn't take her long to get a few bites. She called me with enthusiasm in her voice. I was nervous because I just knew that she was about to present me with either a high six-figure or million dollar deal (I was supremely optimistic). To my dismay, the deal she was excited about was with a medium sized publishing house that was really interested in me. My agent went on to explain that she had negotiated a deal with this particular publishing house as well as another, sort of like a bidding war, but this particular publisher offered a better deal. My agent was so excited, she definitely assumed that I'd accept the offer. It definitely wasn't what I expected and unfortunately, the deal was mediocre to me. Let's be clear, I understood that the distribution channels that the publishing house possessed would be massively larger than mine. However it wasn't large enough for me to surrender total creative control of my work. Therefore, I rejected the deal and continued to evolve in the beautiful world of self-publishing.

Again, my story is my own. You may self-publish and then later on in your career, find a literary agent that secures a deal that takes your career to new heights. If trying to get published is the route you choose, then you should be submitting query letters to agents so that they can shop your books to publishers and find the best deal to get you signed.

If getting published is your goal, prepare to wait for an answer. Sometimes it can take months for a publisher to get back to you. It's an extremely grueling process but you never know what might happen so keep an open mind. Not everyone will see your vision. But you must learn to be okay with that. There are definitely pros and cons to both lanes. The choice is yours. In making this decision, you are either placing your career in your own hands by self-publishing, or placing your career in the hands of a publisher who will take total creative control of your work, but will put it in front of a built-in audience immediately.

Let's talk about the pros of being self-published vs. being published. If you are self-publishing, you get to choose your book cover, editor, make your own decisions and set your own release date. If you sign with a traditional publishing house, they will have full creative control over your book cover, use their in-house editors and release your book six to eighteen months after you sign your contract. Self-publishing allows you to set your own prices and have full control over your royalties which means you pay yourself minus the percentage sites like Amazon or Barnes and Noble take for their publishing services. You don't have to wait for a publisher to issue you a check in which publishing companies will normally pay you for your royalties twice a year (smaller companies may pay more frequently). When you self-publish, you will get paid every month.

Some of the cons about being self-published vs. being published are that you don't have to struggle to find your demographic. Traditional publishing houses generally know who to target and market your book to before they publish you, which is why your book was attractive to them in the first place. When you self-publish, you must start from scratch and build a demographic that caters to your writing, your genre and your brand. If making a career out of being a writer and starting your own publishing company isn't your thing, by all means, search for a publishing house so that they can do the work for you. Maybe you are a talented writer who just wants to get your book in the hands of the masses and you don't want to put in much effort. Signing with a publisher may be the route for you.

By being signed to a large publishing house, you are placing your work in the hands of a machine that will do much of the work for you as far as the publishing process. They will get your books into book stores and take care of marketing your work. I still encourage Authors that are signed to publishing houses to grind hard as far as marketing yourself and your book to assist with the power of the machine. Publishers love to see Authors working as hard as they are and it could actually help secure you a second deal. When you self-publish, that's all you will find yourself doing is grinding, hustling, marketing and advertising because you are pushing a product that you want consumers to read and a brand that you want to embed in the mind of readers to create lasting customers.

Whatever choice you decide to make, be sure to be realistic with yourself. If you have the time to put in to create a business from scratch, which is essentially what self-publishing is, it can be very profitable. If you don't have the desire to put in the work, and your decision is to sign with a major, you may be one of the lucky ones to secure a successful advance and allow the machine to work for you. You can always try self-publishing once your contract is up.

‖ Chapter 8

Publishing

So let's say your decision is to self-publish. Your book has been edited and it's packaged to sell. You should be ecstatic right now, because you've worked hard. Go ahead and pat yourself on the back! You are on your way. Now it's time to set a release date and officially publish your book.

As I mentioned previously, you must have your manuscript formatted for platforms such as Amazon/Barnes and Noble/Create Space/Smashwords or whichever distributing channel you choose to use. Your editor should have done most of the formatting for you. Beware of solicitors trying to take your money to format your book for these platforms. After three rounds of editing (3 rounds is typical for most editorial services), your editor should have sent you back a final version of your manuscript that is formatted for an e-book upload as well as a formatted version of your book for the printers. It all depends on what kind of deal you worked out with your editor. Some editors will format your book to be uploaded as an e-book but will suggest that you acquire a typesetter to format your book for print. If your editor is not skilled in this area at all, you can always format your book to be uploaded into an e-book yourself. Just follow the guidelines provided by the sites and review the drafts until it's to your liking. Believe me, after you publish a few books, formatting your e-books will be a piece of cake.

To upload your manuscript onto an e-book platform for publishing, simply head over to Amazon and/or Barnes and Noble, create an account and follow the prompts to self-publish your book on their platform. Be sure that your synopsis has also been edited because this is going to be your sales pitch. You will enter your synopsis in the book *description* category and double check to see if it's error free. Remember, editors can also drop the ball so you must be proactive in checking for errors.

Now that your book is uploaded and it's ready to sell, it's time to talk about an important piece of self-publishing. Pricing. This is where you need to be strategic. I'm sure a lot of you have saw some of your favorite books on Amazon for $0.99 cents and you thought to yourself, *why is it so cheap?* Well, it's cheap because the Author is being strategic. Especially if it's a first time writer and even better when it's a first time Author writing a series. Let me explain the method to the pricing madness. For a fiction book priced at $0.99 cents on Amazon, that means that the Author will only take home $0.35 cents for each unit sold. Sounds like pennies right? Well it is. You can buy yourself a cup of coffee or some candy from the store for $0.99 cents. Which is why the price point is a wise form of marketing and I'll explain why.

Let's say John Doe is a new Author who no one has ever heard of. John Doe let his family and friends read his book and it's been stamped with the highest of praises. Well not a single person in the literary world has heard of John Doe and the easiest way he can get his name out there is by pricing his book low. Readers are more willing to take a chance on a new Author if they have a great title, cover and their book is affordable. Not to mention John Doe has a part two and three to this series which he plans to release later. Boom, part one was priced so low that consumers are buying it and reviewing it with five star praises and the word of mouth on how great John's book is, is spreading fast. Now the anticipation of part two is growing and John has gained new readers just by making a wise price point call.

Some may argue that this is selling yourself short, however from a business standpoint, it's like spending marketing dollars without spending marketing dollars sort of speak. By pricing your book so low, you have saved money in marketing because by pricing it low, the pricing decision is marketing your book for you. You understand? People are taking a chance on your work because of the price and when they like it, they come back for more. Now John Doe can set a higher price for the next two parts of his series. A good price point would be $2.99 for part two and $5.99 for part three.

When you sell an e-book for $2.99 or more, Amazon will give you, 70% of your sales. Sounds attractive right? I'm sure it must sound better than the $0.35 cents John Doe was getting for his first book. Readers are now more willing to buy the next part of a series after the first book blew them away. You see what happened there? By John pricing his book at a low price, he strategically grew an audience, raised the price on the next part of his series and now John is making great money off of his sales and building his readership.

Another great feature that's offered on Amazon, is the pre-order feature. You can set a release date, upload your book cover and manuscript to Amazon and start promoting ahead of time. This will help you to start building the hype about your book and catch the attention of new readers. You can list your release date on your website, social media platforms and put out teasers to keep people interested. This also helps with eliminating you putting off your book to be published because you have already set the stage for a hard date for your book to be published. An extra push is always needed. The best thing about pre-ordering is pre-sales! Who wouldn't want to see sales for a book that hasn't even been published yet, right?

Once your release date arrives and your book is available for purchase, you are officially an Author! Your work will be an official published document and you can now let your friends, colleagues and family know that you are a published Author. Once you upload your book to Create Space or whatever paperback channel you decide to use to publish your paperbacks, that's when you can physically put your books in the hands of your supporters. That moment will feel like magic! Especially when you sign your first autograph.

Alright, on to discuss publishing paperbacks and wise price points. I personally recommend Create Space or Lightning Source to print your books because you can purchase your own books for as low as $4.00 and sell them for $15.00-$20.00 dollars online. As a self-published Author, pricing your book is a decision that is completely up to you. But again, you must be strategic. When I'm on the road, I find myself selling my paperbacks for $10.00 and sometimes even three-for-fifteen when I'm selling one of my 3-part series. You have to look at it like this, I purchased the books for about $4.00 each so I set a price to ensure that I'm profiting even if it's not substantial. Say I want to sell my books for $5.00 at a book signing, that's only a $1.00 profit, however I gained a new customer, my website is printed on the customer's book and if the reader likes it, they will buy my other paperback books online for $15.00 or check out one of my ebooks. Regardless, I have a potential new reader.

The mistake that I often see with new Authors when I'm on the road is that they price their books to high. They spend money to travel to attend book signings or book expos and try to sell their books for $20.00 and wonder why they have only sold two books and how veteran or strategic Authors have sold out their tables. I'll tell you how, that's because they are not pricing their product properly. The goal is to make money and in making money you have to make smart business decisions. If you print your book for $4.00 each and you try to sell them for $20.00, that's an $18.00 profit. Don't get me wrong, that's great, and it can be attainable if it's your own event. But it's not realistic when you are in a competitive environment, especially for new Authors.

I've seen Authors walk away from expos discouraged because they haven't sold any of their paperbacks. The key is to price your books strategically, I can't stress this enough. If you print your books for $4.00, why not sell them for $5, $10 or $15? That's a $1.00-$11.00 profit. Remember, you have to keep your competitors in mind at all times. You will have competitors at book signings, expos as well as online that's trying to hustle their product as well. Price your product moderately so that it competes, but you also profit.

So we talked about publishing for self-published Authors, let's talk about being published by a traditional publishing house. The good news is, they do all of the uploading on all of the distribution channels for you, so that part is out of your hands. Traditional publishers also use their own editors so you don't have to worry about going over all of the editing drafts. What you should be doing once your publishing company gives you the green light, sets your release date and issues your book cover is to start promoting. You should be getting the word out that you have a book coming out soon. It's very attractive to a publisher when they see the Author working hard to help with promoting awareness to your new release.

Keep in mind, your publisher will be in charge of setting your release date and the pricing of your books. You will have no input on how much your book will be priced at once it's on the market. Also, some publishers will list in their contract, a certain amount of free books offered to the Author when your book is released. Others will offer you discounts at which you can purchase your books from your publisher to use at book signings and other promotional events. Most of the publishing decisions will not be in your control when you sign with a traditional publishing company. However, if you decide to publish or self-publish, be sure to know that the publishing and promotion process does not end once your book is released. That's just the beginning.

‖ Chapter 9

Targeting Your Audience

With the help of Social Media, targeting your audience has never been easier. The use of narrow search engines has helped tremendously. For instance, on Instagram, you can filter searches generically or add in the use of hashtags or type in names to find people directly. Using this method can help you target your audience as well as find out the cities they live in, where they frequent and what they like. These are specifics you will need in order to get your audience to engage in your content.

Before we get into how useful social media can be for targeting, let's first talk about the audience that you already have. Your built-in network. Even if it's only your family and friends, that's the start of your platform. You have obviously done something besides be a great friend or family member to make them become fans and to follow the things that you are doing. What you want to do is immolate this process once your audience grows. In the meantime, keep your inner network engaged, keep your content fresh and answer their needs. Eventually they will start genuinely sharing your work and promoting you without you having to tell them to.

So you have your inner network in place and it's time to expand. One secret that I like to offer is to study your direct competitors closely. When I say study them closely, you have to borderline stalk their work. Sounds silly, but you are now a brand and every brand must research their competitors to understand what they have to do to stand out. This is essentially research. Visit their social media, websites and read their blogs. There's obviously a reason why they have such a large audience. There is something about them that made their readers gravitate towards their work and remain loyal customers. They have discovered their niche and now it's time for you to discover yours.

Once you find out what your niche is, now it's time for you to become an expert at your niche, master it and own it. If you are writing a nonfiction book on the best methods of traveling and being a traveling connoisseur. Traveling is most likely your niche. You should be posting pictures of yourself at the places you've traveled to, interacting with the different cultures and keeping your posts interesting.

By doing this, you are adding a piece of yourself to your brand. Remember, although you have a product, you are a brand as well, and you must sell yourself. What I mean is, you need to make people want to be like you, want to live your life, go the places you go and see the things that you see. That's what keeps them intrigued and that's how you create their "Need" for wanting to follow your work outside of purchasing your products.

Also, discover a secondary skill within you to keep your audience engaged. For instance, I write urban fiction books and not to toot my own horn, but I'd say that I write some pretty great books. But I also know that great books alone is not what's going to keep my audience around waiting for me to publish my next book. I have to feed their needs in the meantime. Which means that I have to constantly create content to keep them wanting to visit my website or social media to see what's next.

One of my secondary passions outside of literature is fashion. I love to dress and I don't miss a chance to post a picture of what I'm wearing on social media. Not to mention, when I researched what my target audience liked, fashion was one of their interests. I've gained new readers just by wearing fashions that I'd wear even if I wasn't online. I get messages asking where'd I get my outfit from and in turn they tell me that they are looking forward to checking out my books as well. Now they'll most likely stick around to see what I'll be wearing next and to check up to see when the next book release is coming out.

Find out what it is inside of you to keep your audience interested and entertained. Consider your audiences taste and expectations. Post videos of yourself speaking to your audience and also talking about some of the things that they are interested in. For example, if you know that your audience engages in the latest reality shows that you also watch, talk about your product in your video and then tell them you have to cut the video short because you have to go watch that particular show. Not only is this humorous but it makes your audience feel like you have a personal connection with them. Your audience will quickly engage in your comments because they'll probably be watching that same show at the same time. The next day you can post up about one of the characters in the reality show you watched and talk about how he or she is similar to one of the characters in your book and ask if they agree. This will get your audience excited about commenting on your post and keep them coming back to see what you'll post next.

Targeting your audience is all about bringing value into the lives of your consumers. What are you doing to add something that they are missing from their lives? Are you providing something that can help change their lives? Are you providing them with tips on love, entertainment or feeding them knowledge? Whatever it is, think outside the box when you create your content so that you can keep them coming back for more.

Once you narrow down your target audience, collect their email addresses and send them a monthly newsletter so that your name and brand stays fresh on their minds. Visuals are important. And lots of people take breaks from social media, however, most people still check their emails frequently. Growing your email list is important because every time you drop a book, one of the first marketing techniques you will use to promote it is sending out an e-blast to your target audience.

When you send out an e-blast, keep your content fresh and consistent with how you present yourself on social media. Nowadays you don't have to be too formal when you talk to your consumers. Most of your customers are there because they liked your personality in the first place. So always stay consistent with your presentation. Keep your material light and fun but professional at the same time.

Research and find out as much as possible about the audience you are marketing to. Speak their language, talk about things they want to hear. And don't be afraid to create intimate relationships with them. What I mean by that is, answer their emails and inboxes and avoid making them feel ignored. Also, engage with your audience when they comment under your posts. That shows them that you are also human and that it's not all about business for you. Remember, your target market is your readership. And essentially they will start telling other people with like-minded interests to also follow you because of how great your product is, how down to earth you are and what you provide. Once you find your target market, it's time to constantly advertise to them.

‖ Chapter 10

Marketing/Advertising

Now let's talk about the biggest misconception of being an Author. It's that you will be rich and famous overnight. Don't we all wish that was the case? Well unfortunately it doesn't work that way. The way it works is that you will get out of it what you put into it. You can definitely generate a hefty income if you hit the industry going full-throttle. If you hit the industry mildly, you can make a comfortable income to bring in some money on the side. It's really up to you, your vision and how hard you work at making a name for yourself. You need the perfect package in order to present your work to an audience. You have to make your audience believe in what you are selling and make sure that they will always return to check and see what you have going on.

Once you become an Author, you are a sales person, you have to be personable, approachable and have a product worth placing in their hands. That means you have to make your readers believe in your product as much as you do. For example, I remember my first book signing. As a newbie, I was naïve and I was blinded by all of the book signings I saw on T.V., and I was sure that my book signing would have the same turn out; a large crowd. I literally thought that there would be a line stacked down the second floor stairwell in the mall layered down into the main lobby. Boy was I wrong!

I was fortunate enough to secure an interview with a radio station beforehand to promote my book signing and I knew for sure that people was going to turn out in massive numbers after hearing me talk about my book. Wrong! Yes, my story might have been compelling and resonated with some of the listeners on the radio, but that didn't matter. Not to mention, I saturated the internet and all of my social media pages with promotion about my book signing. But again, I was a new Author. Yes I was getting great reviews by my new found readers, but I wasn't a household name, nor did I have a buzz that would make readers rush to the mall to meet me.

I had to be real with myself and realize that I was a *nobody* at the time. I was still someone who had to grind to make others believe in me. So as I set up my table in the bookstore, placing my books onto small easels, spread my fancy book marks and post cards all over the table and looked up at the balloons floating up at the ceiling that the book store provided for me, I smiled. As I stood in front of the decorated table, I turned around to discover not one single reader waiting there to greet me. I immediately became discouraged, but that burning desire to make readers believe in me sparked the inner hustler inside of me.

I scooped up the postcards off of the table and made it my duty to get it into the hands of each and every one who entered the book store or walked by my table in the mall. Mind you, my book is fiction and my genre wasn't popular at the time. Therefore, convincing people to check out my book instead of picking up a how-to book or the late Michael Jackson's Memoir was a challenge. However, it was a challenge that I happily accepted.

I will never forget, there was a beautiful, slender woman with blonde hair and an arm full of romance novels standing in front of my table, eyeing my books. I smiled at her and handed her my post card. She casually browsed at the front and back of it and I could literally see the doubt written in her expression. I'm sure she didn't read past the title, "A Hood Chick's Story" because it didn't sound anything like a romance novel, which is obviously the genre she was interested in reading. She took a deep breath and placed my post card back on my table and I was offended. I couldn't believe she didn't even want to at least keep the post card, I mean, it was free!

Finally she asked me the golden question. "Well, I normally don't read books like this, tell me why I should buy your book?" Her question shook me up and I was stuck in my seat. I wasn't expecting such a simple, yet complex question, I mean, I was a newbie. I was used to telling people what my book was about and then I sold them on my synopsis. I never had to explain *why* they should purchase my book. I felt completely challenged. It was at that very moment that I realized that I had to sell myself beyond what my book was about and to also sell my readers an experience. It was only fair that I shared with her the very reason she should add my book to her collection.

With confidence, I picked up one of my books off the table and I cracked it open to the first page. I smiled and nodded to the books she had tucked under her arm. "Well I noticed that you are picking up some romance novels. Not only does my book consist of romance but it also consists of characters that can speak and relate to you, your family, friends and I can guarantee that reading, "A Hood Chick's Story" alone will be more like watching a movie rather than reading a book. There are instances in this book that are life changing. It's actually based on my personal story and struggles. It'll tug on your heartstrings but it will without a doubt have you craving for part two." She giggled and said, "Craving huh?" I repeated it, "Yes, craving." Then I proceeded to tell her that part two would be dropping the following month because of the high demand for updates on the characters in part one. Boom, she was sold and she immediately purchased my book. I made sure that I exchanged social media contacts with her and asked her to leave a review after she finished reading it. Needless to say, I secured a long term customer. I was able to sell her, not only on what my content was about, but *why* she should purchase it. I even made her laugh and laughter is always a great selling point.

Soon after that purchase, I found my sales pitch. I snatched my postcards off of my table and not only did I hand them out, but now I was putting it in their hands and telling them *why* they should buy my book at the same time. That's all it took, that was my intro. After that, they would stop and skim at the synopsis on the back of my book, read the first page and then I'd secure a new customer. I repeated this pattern by talking to each and every person that I handed a postcard to. Once someone saw me pitching to one customer, others would naturally come to my table to see what the hype was about and before I knew it, my table was crowded with people buying books and I happily signed them, took pictures with them and made sure that I told them to leave me a review once they've read it.

Now back to me living in fairytale land and assuming that all of my book signings would be full of readers knocking each other over just to meet me and purchase my books. Yes, that was a pure comical and I was definitely ahead of myself. I definitely learned the hard way but it was worth it. Having people waiting for me to sign their books and awaiting my arrival didn't happen until later on in my career. In the beginning, most of my next book signings went exactly as I described above since I had no real following at the time. I had a lot of people that read and loved my book but I needed more word of mouth, more marketing and more placements of my books in the stores before I had people knocking down the doors to see little ole' me.

I have to shout out all of the readers that doubted my book because although my genre wasn't their speed, they gave it a chance. For that I'm grateful. For example, the slender blonde woman who took a chance on me at my first book signing which whom I'm still friends with today by the way. Customers that don't normally read books in your genre will sing your praises if they tried your book and enjoyed it. Their reviews will usually read similar to this:

"Now normally this isn't the genre that I normally read, but I could really see a lot of myself in the main character. This story really hit home for me and I got emotional a few times. Now I'm addicted to this series. Thanks for making me a new urban fiction fan LaShonda."

The power in a review like that is priceless. You ever hear of the saying, *A little goes a long way?* Well it's true. A small review like that can help your doubters pick up your novel and give your book a try. That's what it's all about, attracting consumers within your demographic as well as attracting readers outside of your normal audience and getting them to believe in your work.

Marketing your books at book signings, expos and book events are a great way to generate income and help expand your brand. You don't have to hire a publicist to get booked at these type of events. I spent thousands of dollars on publicists in the past when I first started becoming successful only to have them land me at events that I could've signed up for myself. You should be using your marketing dollars on more strategic promotion, not a publicist. Such as finding a graphic designer to create flyers for all of your book events so that when you post your events or book signing online, the post looks professional, polished and attractive to your consumers. The goal is to get them to come to your event so that they can purchase your work. And investing in the right designers can help you stand out from the crowd.

Utilize Facebook, Instagram and Google to locate book festivals and expos in your area or in other cities. The internet is so rich with content and in depth information, you can find anything by doing your research. Once you locate these events, they'll usually list all of the information needed to sign up for a table to attend. But remember, the goal is to make money so don't sign up for each and every event you find online.

If there is a book festival in Texas and you live in Boston, your plane ticket might be $500.00, your hotel may cost $200.00 for the weekend and the cost of your table at the event may be $250.00. That's $950.00, not including the cost of your meals. When creating your marketing plan, ask yourself if events like these are worth it. Will you make over $1000.00 in sales when you get to Texas? If you are a new Author, the answer is, not likely. So if you are a new Author and you are planning a tour, be sure to schedule events that are closer to where you live so that the amount you spend on these events makes sense. The goal is to make money, not lose any.

Now pay very close attention to how payment at book signings work. Okay, if you know of any mom and pop stores in your city, be sure to establish relationships with the owners. Normally book stores in your city are the first stores to put your books on their shelves. Some hold your book on consignment, which I don't recommend and some will cut you a check for a certain amount of books on the spot. Be prepared to take a 50-60% loss. Yes you heard me right. That discount is the norm when book stores or distributors buy your books in bulk.

I used to be offended and feel like I was getting robbed when I heard about the 50-60% discount on paperbacks, but I discovered this was the norm across the board. And I'd rather have a check cut for me on the spot from book stores rather than offering my books on consignment. The reason I'm against consignment is because I've had my own horror stories from personal experience. Some of the stores that I've had these encounters with are out of business right now. They were located in New York City and New

Jersey and they'd send me invoices to order large quantities of my books on consignment. In the beginning, they made good on their word and used to send me checks for thousands of dollars once my books were sold. Eventually, the checks started bouncing and I've had conversations that I'd hate to repeat to you when I called to demand my payments. I mean, this is my money and my hard work that we are talking about. To this very day, these stores owe me thousands of dollars. However, as I explained before, everything I've done in this business was through trial and error. I didn't look at this situation as if I took a loss. I look at it as if I spent marketing dollars because although these stores didn't pay me for the books that they've sold, my books are still in the hands of hundreds of readers in that market. As I stated before, I've made many mistakes in this industry so that you won't have to. With that being said, say no to consignment, lol.

Back to book signings. When you set up a book signing inside of bookstore like Barnes and Noble, if Ingram is one of your distributors, then they would have most likely already ordered books from Ingram for your book signing. That means that all you have to do is arrive. However, don't expect to be paid at the end of your signing. They have already purchased your books through your distributor for the 50-60% discount so your payment will come later. Keep that in mind when you schedule to travel for signings in these type of book stores. I always use signings like these for promotional purposes and I only do them locally.

If you want to be paid at the end of your book signing, be sure that it's a store where you have to bring your own books with you to sell. After you sell your books, you give the store owner a cut and you walk away with cash. This is the same course of action for a book festival or expo. You will pay for your table, bring your own books, but you will keep all of the cash you earn.

The entire time that you are at a book signing, keep in mind that you are marketing yourself. Make sure that you purchase material that reflect your brand and make sure that it stands out. For example, I have a large banner that I bring with me to book signings with my picture and contact information on it. I also have a table cloth branded with my publishing company, book covers and slogans from my website. Painting visuals is everything. When readers who couldn't make your signings see pictures of your book signings online, you want to make them wish that they were there to meet you.

Now let's talk about online marketing/promotion and advertising. Set up a campaign ahead of time so that when it's release day, you already know what you have to do. For instance, structure your e-blast in advance, write out all of the content that you want included in it so that when your book is live on Amazon, all that you have to do is copy the link into your e-blast and send it off. Same goes for Facebook and Instagram advertising posts. Choose a picture of your book cover, a trailer of your book or some sort of promotional visual you want to use for advertising your book in advance so that when it's release day, you will post the promotional content under your picture along with the link to where they can purchase it. Having all of this queued up in advance can make your life easier.

Also, place excerpts on your social media outlets so that your readers can see a sneak peek of what they can expect in your new book. Make them hungry to want to crave what you are serving. Ask them to share the excerpts with their friends and book clubs as well. Book clubs are an essential part of your career. I definitely recommend that you become a member of as many online book clubs as possible. They love to promote new releases.

If you are unclear on the vision of your book, your marketing efforts will fall flat. You must become a storyteller through social media. Tell your demographic what's in it for them. Your content should sell the story of your brand, clarify what you are sharing and determine what compels your readers.

Be sure to network with your fellow Authors and don't be afraid to enlist the help of others. Genuinely show your fellow Authors that you support them and in turn, they will support you.

Some will even post and share your book when they see you on your grind. Be sure to do the same for them. Present yourself as a colleague instead of a competitor. If you appear as a competitor, they may be more reluctant to embrace you. But I guarantee when you begin to network with Authors and start creating your own lane, they will gravitate towards you and start to try to study what you are doing that they aren't. That's your goal, to surpass Authors that you once looked up to and I believe that you can do it!

Another great marketing tactic are giveaways. When your book drops, set up an engaging contest. Post up a question for your readers relating to the title of your book and tell them to drop their answer along with their email addresses in your comments so that you can give a gift copy of your book to the winner. What you are also doing here is collecting new email addresses to add to your e-blast.

Giveaways are important because not only do your readers feel like you are being generous but they also feel like you care. Who doesn't want a free book, right? Your readers will be appreciative and you'll seem more human to them. Other fun giveaways are Kindles, personalized notebooks or pens with your name and brand on them because although these are giveaways, you are marketing yourself. Don't forget to tell them to take a picture with their free gift once they receive it. And they will most likely leave you a review for your generosity.

Let's talk a little bit more about reviews for a moment. I'm often asked if bad reviews can hurt sales. The simple answer to that question is yes. Some consumers buy books based solely on reviews. However, the greater majority buy books because of the title despite what the reviewers have to say. Actually, all reviews are good reviews. I know you probably just re-read that last sentence to see if I typed it right but you read it correctly. Even bad reviews are good reviews. Why? Because online book stores such as Amazon and Barnes and Noble flag books based on activity. If you have a good book and the majority of your reviews are five stars and a small percentage of your books are one or two star reviews, Amazon recognizes that your book is being read and it stays in circulation. No, we may never understand the machine behind Amazon, Barnes and Noble, etc., but based on experience, this is what is theorized and what I've learned to be true.

After you drop your book, tell your readers to like and share it. You can set up contests to give the person with the most shares a $20.00 Amazon gift card. Think outside the box so that your readers can promote for you. Set up strategic marketing so that your consumers are helping you spread the word. You need your link in front of as many readers as possible.

Focus on advertising to your market. Use ad campaigns to target your audience and set activity goals. Pay attention to your engagement and provide great customer service by interacting.

Develop a strategy to collect more emails and also social media names. Use the social media names to tag your audience when you are posting content that you know that they'll enjoy. They will appreciate this. Also list your products on your website and social media. If you have attracted a new consumer, they must see everything that you are selling to see what the most attractive item is for them to buy. Satisfy their needs not their wants and in your case they *need* to want to read your book. You must structure a campaign to show them *why* they need it. Invest in yourself and create your own lane so that you can stand out to your consumers. Use creative YouTube videos, skits, whatever you find that is making them come back for more, do it! At the same time, continue to scout out your competition and be better than them!

Other smart online marketing is leaving comments under other Author's blogs or YouTube channels with your knowledge on the subject they are speaking about. Be sure not to leave comments asking their fans to go buy your book. Leave comments pertaining to your knowledge and know-how on the subject at hand, and they will become interested and in turn check you out. Same goes for other Author's social media posts. Leave comments cheering them on.

Here's an example:

"Hey fellow Author, I definitely agree with you on this subject, I wrote about the same topic in my blog last week."

Seems sort of sneaky but it's actually strategic. You will find that quite a few of the people on that particular Author's thread will come over and check you out.

Join sites such as Good Reads, AuthorsDen and Smashwords (FYI- you can use Smashwords to upload your manuscript to the iBook platform). You need to make sure that your book is on as many free online sites as possible. The good news is, sometimes you may browse a site such as Good Reads and discover that your book is already placed on the platform. That's right, your readers will sometimes create these pages for you. When this happens, you should pat yourself on the back because that means that readers felt that your book was so good, that there was a need to share it with other readers.

When I went over to create my Good Reads page, I had discovered all of my books were already on the platform with hundreds of reviews as well as readers recommending them to other readers. I was ecstatic! Not only because they placed my books on this platform but because I had found a place where readers lived and how they felt about my books.

Now let's get into advertising. Advertisement can be pricey but it's beneficial. You can purchase ads on Facebook and Instagram and cater it to your target market. Take advantage of the filters. If you are writing a book about fitness, filter your ads to target fitness gurus, their fan pages, fitness products and any other relevant topic or name that will help narrow your ads to your target market.

When you are a new Author, don't spend too much money on ads, play around with different target markets by spending a small amount of money before you find which market works. Ads are a great way to keep your book in front of people with similar interests. Be sure that there is a link in your ad that a consumer can click on that will lead them straight to make a purchase. The link should take them somewhere to lead to revenue off your social media.

If you have a significant amount of marketing dollars to spend, then by all means, create ads on Facebook and Instagram starting at a price point of $20.00 to $100.00 a day. Filter your target market appropriately and watch your sales climb. The good news is, you can view your sales on Amazon and Barnes and Noble in a graph. You can watch what days your sales peaked and what days they fell short and determine which one of your marketing tactics have been working. Also, if you really have a large cushion of advertising dollars to work with, advertise your books with individuals with large social media followings that cater to your fanbase. This is one of the smartest ways to grow your following and increase your sales.

The goal of advertising and promoting your book is to attract new readers and generate sales. You must be persistent in your marketing and advertising approach. You should be promoting your book even before its release date. Create a countdown campaign so that your readers are excited about your release. Come up with crafty content for them to share. For instance, you can post your book cover and tell your readers to share it on as many platforms as possible. On the day of your release, tell them that the first three people to screenshot their purchase of your book and how many pages they shared your content on, will win a $50.00 prize. Make readers want to help you spread the word of your book. The reach of your readers go a long way.

‖ Chapter 11

Time to Make That Money!

Whew! It's been a long journey but you've pushed through. You were disciplined enough to finish your book, publish it and put it on the market. Now it's time to discuss making the most money out of your product. Of course by using relevant keywords on Amazon when you publish your e-book will help Amazon to recognize your book as being amongst the popular titles. The secret is to insert keywords from some of the title of the books that are on the top ten Best Sellers lists. This will help the platform recognize your book and put it on the forefront along with the popular titles for readers to see. If this is done correctly, you can definitely hit a sales peak and see your book listed next to some of the Best Selling titles.

There was a point in time that the Barnes and Noble's Nook e-book platform was very popular. My books did extremely well on the Nook platform and I was generating around $5-10k per month off of my Nook sales. However, I was making double that amount on Kindle, which brings me to my next point. It seems as if Kindle has trumped Nook e-books over the years. The choice is entirely up to you if you'd like to upload your e-books on Amazon (kindle) or

Barnes and Noble (nook) or both. Let me let you in on a secret that can possibly get you the most profit; especially as a new writer. If you publish your e-book exclusively on Amazon for 90 days and enroll it into KDP Select and KOLL, (Kindle Owner's Lending Library) database, you will get a cut out of the KOLL budget each month and as it stands, the KOLL Global Fund is at 21 million dollars.

No, you will not be getting a million dollars out of the budget but at least you will be generating free dollars just by keeping your books exclusively on Amazon. That means that you can't publish your e-book on any other digital platform for 90 days. If you are unsure if this is the route for you, upload your first book on both Amazon and Barnes and Noble first. Thereafter, publish your second e-book exclusively on Amazon and enroll it into KDP Select to see if it's worth it. I'd also like to add that by enrolling your book into KDP select, you are also making your book available on International markets as well. When I ever found out that I had a following Internationally, I was elated! I'm telling you, you couldn't tell me nothing. I was no longer just a local Author, I was international and I gloated for weeks when I saw my first International sales. It's a feeling that you want to share with others. It's like a dream you can't be awoken from. The good news is, that all of this is achievable for you. You too can obtain an audience that reaches past your targeted demographic and you too can win in these markets! If your marketing and advertising is done correctly, you can generate a ton of income from e-book sales alone.

Now let's get into how you can generate income off of your paperback books. The evolution of e-books has unfortunately caused an abundance of bookstores to close down. Many great relationships that I've acquired over the years with bookstore owners have unfortunately came to an end because of the demise of their bookstores. It was definitely a sad time for the book industry. One of the book stores that my books thrived in was Borders and I was sad when they closed down. That being said, with the market being mostly digital based, you will probably make more money off of your e-books sales rather than your paperback sales.

This isn't bad news at all because the income can be awesome. I remember I told myself that when I started making six figures off of my e-book sales, that I would quit my job. And that's exactly what happened. My advertising and marketing campaigns were structured so well, that I was able to build an audience that trusted the work that I published and in turn, I made a ton of money. With e-books helping tons of Authors quit their jobs and become full-time writers, this is the exact reason why many Authors only publish e-books rather than paperbacks. But I want you to capitalize off of both.

When you publish an e-book, the cost is totally free. However, when you publish a paperback, you must acquire a typesetter and pay your graphic designer to format your book for the printers. And then you have to purchase your own books to sell at book signings. Many Authors avoid this process since they make more money off of their online book sales. As I stated before, I recommend publishing your books on both e-book and paperback formats and I'll tell you why.

First of all, every new Author should go on tour. You should travel and establish relationships with bookstore owners and meet new readers. That being said, you can't bring your digital books with you on tour and sign it for your readers. What product will you sell when you get to your book signings? Your paperbacks will make you money when you travel! Also, you must not neglect those readers that still get pleasure out of holding a paperback book in their hands. Be sure to cater to the entirety of your audience and get out there and network. Just like the old saying goes, you have to shake hands and kiss babies. Networking in person is a huge part of becoming a Best Selling Author.

Also, if you are an expert in a particular field, writing a book that outlines your expertise is essential to your success. Having paperbacks available at your speaking engagements are critical for your brand. If you are selling information or you're building a brand, there is usually a message behind your story and your book can help you sell that message. Your concept should bring influence and supersede other competitive brands on the market.

Branding yourself is extremely important. Your website should be your penname.com (example: www.lashondadevaughn.com). Be sure to place your social media and contact information on all of your marketing material and on your website. The beauty of e-books is that readers now have the capability to click on the link to all of your social media pages directly from the inside of your e-book. They can also click on the link to your website and sign up for your newsletters.

Your social media sites should also be named after your pen name to keep your brand consistent. Create hashtags using your pen name and don't miss a chance at mentioning your brand when you are promoting. Create memes geared toward what you are writing about because readers are more likely to share content like this. Be sure that your social media name is branded on the meme as well. Get your readers excited about what you are writing. Start friending likeminded individuals on social media that are interested in your focus. Make this process fun. When you start making money off of your passion, it no longer feels like work.

Other ways to make money in publishing besides selling your e-books and paperbacks are to monetize your blogs. You are now a writer, so when you create your website, include a page for blogging. Connect that blog page to your google account so that you can monetize your page. You can also monetize products outside of your books by creating memorable quotes and passages in your books for your readers to remember.

For example, in my book, "A Hood Chick's Story," I used the slogan, *Don't Cry Just Ride* in the last chapter of my book. This was an actual quote from my little brother that he had said weeks before he died. He said that if he ever passed away, don't cry for him, just ride for him. In my book, I told my readers what that slogan meant to me. To me it meant that I shouldn't spend my days sulking but that I should be riding this wave called life and discovering my purpose. To my surprise, my readers were hash-tagging that slogan. Some were even getting tattoos of the slogan and tagging me in it. I couldn't believe how much influence the words in my books held. That's when I knew that I had to provide my readers with more than just books. I got hats and T-shirts made with *Don't cry, Just ride* printed on them in all colors and they were selling like hot cakes. There are multiple ways to ensure that you get the most revenue out of your product, you just have to discover what it is that readers love about your work.

Be persistent in your efforts. If you have a slogan or some sort of theme in your book that most of your readers mention in your reviews or comments, use that theme to create a buzz. If you wrote a book about women's rights and you constantly mentioned, *women are warriors* in your book, turn it into a campaign. Start a *Women are Warriors* campaign or foundation and watch how many of your readers will start championing for you.

There are many ways to make money in publishing. If you are an expert or a thought leader, provide coaching or consulting services. Your book is the Segway into making clients believe that they are in great hands with someone who has written a book on their expertise, and they will trust you. And in turn, feel comfortable spending money on your services. Speaking engagements are also a great way to make money from this industry. At the end of your engagement, you will have an audience full of people that will most likely purchase your books. Also, becoming a ghostwriter is another means of making money in publishing. Many ghostwriters get paid handsomely for writing books for other people. I know quite a few ghostwriters that make a comfortable living off of ghostwriting.

Many Authors don't realize how much power they have in writing a book and how they can capitalize off of their words. You are now a content creator, a professional and someone that people admire. Your book is what attracted your clients to you in the first place. The power of your words and imagination have created something that became enlarged because of something that you had to say, and it can take you places that you've never dreamed of.

"Logic will get you from A-Z, imagination will take you everywhere."- Albert Einstein

‖ Chapter 12

Keep Going

After you have published your book, made some money and effectively produced your marketing plan down to a science, you must KEEP GOING! It's easy to get comfortable and complacent once you achieve your desired results, but you must remember your readers are watching you. They will constantly wonder, what's next? And you must always answer their needs and provide them with what that next big "thing" is. Rather it's a book or a product that you have created from your content. Keep chasing the next thing and make it bigger than your last project.

Seeing your books in bookstores, signing autographs and meeting the needs of your consumers will give you a rush like no other. You must seize the moment because it's precious and you've worked hard to develop your platform. If you stay consistent, you can watch your empire bloom into its highest potential. You've nurtured your baby from the womb and now you have to tools to ensure that it continues to grow in abundance. Keeping that momentum is extremely important.

Now let's recap and get into some tips to keep you motivated so that you'll keep going and keep growing!

We've learned that three phases of writing will always need to be addressed when writing a book:

- **The Title Phase:** Making your title competitive with the titles in your genre and placing it on an equally competitive book cover.

- **The Story Phase:** Combatting writer's block by using some of the previously mentioned techniques. Utilize the useful methods of forcing out your ideas such as an outline, writing your synopsis, or free-writing. Ensure that you flush out your story to its entirety and abandon the procrastination boat. Feel free to join writer's groups, start your own book club and post samples of your writing on your website. You must do what you must to keep your creativity in front of you to avoid putting your writing off. Don't get caught in the Rewind Game (re-writing and re-reading). Keep writing until you finish! Use logic and imagination and create a classic.

- **The Ending Phase:** We've learned solid tips to avoid leaving abrupt cliffhangers. We've also learned that your ending will determine your review. If your book was great but your ending was mediocre, your readers will leave you a mediocre review. Tie up all loose ends and leave no questions unanswered when ending your book. Always end your book leaving your reader with something to think about long after they've finished reading your story.

Now let's recap what we've learned about marketing and advertising. You must be working on these areas in advance. Remember you are branding yourself, so you must stay consistent in your efforts:

Social Media – Consistency is key! Post content on each of your social media platforms every day. Websites such as Hootsuite can help you manage all of your social media platforms in one place. This will save you time so that you can focus on other areas of marketing.

- Engage Readers on live chats at least once every two weeks.
- Start a YouTube channel, begin Vlogging and constantly showing visuals to your readers to keep them engaged.
- Understand the riches in the niches and create your secondary niche to keep your readers coming back.
- Create content that your readers will like and share.

Marketing and Advertisement – Discover your target market and start focusing on their needs. Record their email addresses, post content with engaging posts and ask them to tag their friends. Market YOURSELF along with your brand. People like real people so be sure to reply to their comments and inboxes and be genuine.

- Give away free material and ask the winner to post a picture when they receive their free gift.
- Create Facebook ads, boost your posts and be sure to narrow your filters to your target audience.
- Understand the power of research and knowing your demographic. Find out what your target market likes to watch, wear and hang out. Cater your content to their specific needs so that they will constantly come back to see what you have going on.
- Identify business concepts that others miss. If you see ten of your favorite Authors doing the same marketing strategies,

discover something that they haven't done and implement it into your marketing plan. This is how you will stand out and create your own lane.

Being a published Author isn't for the faint of hearts. You mustn't have a cavalier attitude when approaching this industry, but instead, an unrelenting passion for this. A humble heart is definitely required for this business because not every day is the same. After you finish your book, you are going to feel completely liberated. That idea to write a book that you had trapped in your head for so long, has finally come into fruition. You'll smile every chance you get and tell everyone from your mom to the man at the grocery store that you've finished your book. You have every right to gloat because you stayed committed and you got it done! This is when you'll take a deep breath and realize, *wow, that wasn't' as bad as I thought.*

Remember to treat your brand like a business and it will be good to you. Work hard and stay persistent and consistent. Once you start generating interest from the media, be sure to keep yourself in order. In the words of Eric Worre, *"your calendar is your boss."* Allow it to keep you in order. Write everything down and follow-up with people who contact you for interviews. Make sure that you stick to your deadlines and be prompt for your interviews, book signings and meetings. Remain professional at all times.

Now I know that you are ready to get out there and make some money off of your hard work. But I just want to leave you with some words of encouragement to keep you fired up to keep going. Stay motivated and set writing and marketing goals for yourself daily. It's so easy for us to get distracted and procrastination is the killer of dreams. I can't stress this enough. Don't let procrastination find you and hold you hostage from achieving your goal of being a writer. Many writers table their great stories only to watch someone else write a similar story and live the life that they wished they were living. Don't let this be you! Let your dream harvest into something great. Avoid the naysayers and don't let them distract you from greatness. There is only one person that has to believe in your dream and that is you!

Watching your competitors climb up the ranks can really discourage you. Please understand that your lane is your own. For example, I've written fourteen books, yes I've managed to reach Best Selling Success on some of the top Best Seller's lists but I've never landed on the New York Times Best Sellers List. But that doesn't mean that I haven't sold hundreds of thousands of books independently. I've made some great money in this industry and never compared my success to others. What I did, was create a solid form of generating income off of my talent and have a loyal following. Don't get me wrong, accolades are great, but what's the average American chasing? Money, right? Now imagine making money off of your passion, it's a win-win situation. But remember, you can chase money, but money will only follow you when you are consistent.

Lastly, keep online and offline support around you. Their support plays a major role in keeping you on track. They will encourage you to put action behind your vision which are both pillars of success, (action and vision). And be sure to make people feel inspired by your story or message. Your book is used as a tool to enhance your message. That in itself will not only attract readers but earn you lifelong readers. Always write with passion and use your authentic voice because your voice is what's going to make your book unique, no matter what genre you are writing in.

If this book is used correctly, you will go from amateur to expert.

If this book is used and applied correctly, you will go from amateur to expert rather quickly. However, you must finish your book first. There is so much wasted information in an unwritten book. Statistics show that out of thousands of aspiring Authors with desires of writing a book, only 1% will actually write one. That in itself should be motivation! Don't remain frozen by thoughts of fear or failure; there is someone waiting to hear what you have to say. Now go write that book and make that money! You got this!

You will never discover your greatness by living in your comfort zone.

-Warren Buffet

Other Titles by LSDV Publications

A Hood Chick's Story 1-3

I'd Rather Be Single 1-3

Love's A Bitch 1-2

If All Men Cheat, All Women Should Too!

When A Woman's Fed Up 1-2

She Got Love For A Bean Town Thug

Side Chick Secrets 1-2

Married But Available

Loving My Thug 1 & 2

No Love Beneath The Bottom Of The Barrel 1-2

The Closer I Get 1-2

Daddy's Baby, Mamas Maybe

Soul Custody

For more information on LaShonda DeVaughn visit:

www.lashondadevaughn.com

Facebook: Author LaShonda DeVaughn

Instagram: lashondadevaughn

Snap: UrFavAuthor

Twitter: @hoodchickstory